PeTA's VEGAN COLLEGE COOKBOOK

PeTA's
VEGAN
COLLEGE COOKBOOK

275 EASY. CHEAP. AND DELICIOUS RECIPES TO KEEP YOU VEGAN AT SCHOOL

PEOPLE FOR THE ETHICAL TREATMENT OF ANIMALS
WITH **STARZA KOLMAN** AND **MARTA HOLMBERG**

SOURCEBOOKS, INC.®
NAPERVILLE, ILLINOIS

Published by Sourcebooks, Inc.
P.O. Box 4410, Naperville, Illinois 60567–4410
(630) 961–3900
Fax: (630) 961–2168
www.sourcebooks.com

Library of Congress Cataloging-in-Publication Data

PETA's vegan college cookbook : 275 easy, cheap, and delicious recipes to keep you vegan at school / by PETA.
      p. cm.
  Includes bibliographical references and index.
  1. Vegan cookery. I. People for the Ethical Treatment of Animals. II. Title: Vegan college cookbook.
  TX837.P5133 2009
  641.5'636--dc22

                                    2009002529

                    Printed and bound in the United States of America.
                                    BG 10 9 8

Dedicated to peta2,
the youth division of People for the
Ethical Treatment of Animals (PETA),
which has been spicing things up since 2002.

CONTENTS

FOREWORD
FROM INGRID E. NEWKIRK, PRESIDENT
OF PETA

When I was young, I went to school in a totally scary boarding convent run by mean nuns who dressed like Darth Vader and gave us food that was like something from a prison. The boarding school was stuck in the Everlasting Snows of the Himalayan Mountains, so it was really pretty if you looked outside the window, but really ugly when you looked down at your plate. Maybe the cooks hated us or something, but we were served weird dishes like hairy okra in white sauce (which I often stuck in my pocket and snuck out of the dining hall, because the nuns made us eat everything or we'd get it again for as many meals as it took for us to finish it). I remember (vividly) a gruel optimistically called "pepper water," which consisted of water, yes, and some chili paste, yes, and tamarind roots. If you have ever had Vegemite and hated it, avoid tamarind root. One day, some of us raided the teachers' kitchen and made off with a can of peaches that we opened with a boat hook. We were so excited. It's a wonder any of us survived.

Striking out on my own didn't improve my food situation much. Being raised in a food environment like that convent was like getting cooking lessons from electric eels. In fact, there was a Dutch girl in my dorm who used to lie awake at night and talk about how much she missed jellied eels. That's probably what first made me think that being a vegetarian sounded pretty good. Anyway, what did I know about cooking? A big, fat nothing. And back then, microwaves were something engineers discussed in science magazines.

So, I learned to boil water and throw things in it and cry a lot. If friends came over, I would cook multiple dishes and take them out of the oven, some burnt, some done, and some raw. That wasn't much fun, but I got invited over to their places a lot, which would have been a cunning plan if it had been a plan.

Later came the hippie food co-ops, where you could actually get things like soy milk but with a slight snag: you had to mix it yourself. Yes, they would sell you soy milk *powder*, and your job was to take it home, find a whisk, and whip it up into something drinkable. I bow down to you, Silk.

So now I live in food heaven. Vegan world. Land of convenience. Home of stuff-yourself-silly-and-still-be-healthy, ethical, happy, and environmentally sane. Thanks to Starza and Marta, who compiled and wrote this book, and the PETA food elves, your dorm life can now be perfect. If something gets you down, just open this book and be comforted within minutes—maybe seconds. And speaking of seconds, yes, please, we'd like some more. Starza, Marta, get cracking on that sequel!

ACKNOWLEDGMENTS

A special thanks to: Rebecca Fischer, Lara Sanders, and Patricia Trostle for their invaluable assistance throughout the entire cookbook writing process. To Dan Shannon, Joel Bartlett, Ryan Huling, Chris Garcia, and P.J. Smith for their guidance and input. To Becky Fenson, Amy Elizabeth, Heidi Parker, and Lindsay Pollard-Post for their amazing ability to capture the college voice. To Blake Simmons and Laura Brown for their organizational and research abilities. To Erin Nevius, Sara Appino, and Carrie Gellin at Sourcebooks, Inc., for their help in making this work come together. And to the following people for lending us their recipes, opinions, and taste buds in order to make this book come to life:

Claire Marlatt, Christine Doré, Rachel Owen, Jennifer Cierlitsky, Alka Chandna, David Perle, Kelly Respess, Paul Kercheval, Chris Holbein, Jenny Lou and Josh Browning, Sean Conner, Caleb Wheeldon, Michael Croland, Teresa Cooper, Christine Tynes, Sarah Pearson, Megan Hartman, Karen Porreca, Patti Tillotson, Meg Caskey, Kelli Provencio, Colleen Higgins, Roxanne Conwell, Jannette Patterson, Julian Carr, Desiree Acholla, Colleen Borst, Jessica Johnston, Jennifer Hurst, Melissa Kessler, Elizabeth O'Mara, Tracy Reiman, Liesel Wolff, Kim DeWester, Travis Poland, Laura Frisk, Kaci Fairbanks, Jenny Woods, Allison Liu, Jessica Jagmin, Carrie Ann Knauss, Katie Smith, Kim Terepka, Anita DeWester, Jessica Roland, Madalyn Grimm, Ashley Byrne, and Libby Simons.

Finally, a big thank you to Ingrid E. Newkirk for trusting us with this project, writing a rockin' foreword, and submitting many, many recipes.

PART ONE

WHAT YOU NEED TO KNOW

IN THE BEGINNING, THERE WAS THE MICROWAVE

You may be wondering why we didn't just make a vegan cookbook that requires a, you know, stove. Well, we know you're busy. After spending hours on end cramming Shakespeare into your head, we're positive that the last thing you want to do is stand in front of a hot stove stirring sauce or waiting for a pot of water to boil. And c'mon—a microwave is so much more accessible than a stove. Microwave in the student union or your dorm room? Check. Stovetop? Not so much.

Microwaved vegan food. Yum! Okay, we're not totally naïve here—we know this probably conjures up an image of a bowl of nuked, wilted kale or some other oh-so-healthy (but possibly gag-inducing) green food. However, at PETA we're all about breaking stereotypes, so we've created a cookbook dedicated to vegan food that doesn't require a stove *and* tastes delicious.

College is supposed to be the time in your life when you're really figuring out how to fend for yourself. You're already trying to figure out physics and how to get out of going to your 8 a.m., so who has time to learn how to flambé or frappé? Did you know you can actually make pasta without a pot or pancakes without a pan? Well, believe it, buddy. We can teach you all you need to know to make simple, effortless meals. You'll have plenty of time later on in life to make friends with your stove.

We're betting you've been there—nuking package after package of ramen. Opening the freezer with your fingers crossed, hoping there's a frozen burrito lurking behind the ice tray. Or gagging down some pizza, trying your hardest not to dwell on the fact that mold makes interesting shapes in a week—anything to put off actually spending time and effort cooking a meal.

That's where we come in.

Why didn't we make a cookbook that's just like every other one out there? Because we love being the black sheep, the lone wolf, the creep in the back corner. Okay, maybe not that last one, but you get the idea. We dare to be different, and we bet you are itchin' to do the same.

HEADS UP

So we know you are old enough and smart enough to know how to work a microwave safely, but we still worry! Please humor us and keep the following in mind when using a microwave:

- Take extreme caution when removing containers of hot food and boiling water from the microwave to avoid spills and burns. Burns don't feel so hot. (Get it?)

- Although most plastic containers are microwave-safe, please double check before putting one in the microwave. When in doubt, use a container that is clearly marked "Microwave Safe" or "Microwaveable."

- Of course, no metal objects in the microwave! You know you don't want to be *that guy*—the person in your dorm or apartment that catches the only working microwave on fire.

Also, FYI, all of these recipes were tested in 700-watt microwaves and heated on the HIGH setting unless otherwise mentioned in the recipe. Cooking times may vary depending on altitude and microwave.

OK, that should cover all of the boring, lecture-y stuff. On to the fun part!

CLIFFS NOTES FOR COOKING

Fake. It's not exactly the word everyone is dying for people to call them, we know. But if you can pull off some delicious, satisfying vegan cooking, you've learned to fake your way into people's stomachs quite well. And if you can get all those crazy "omnis" (which is much nicer than calling them "meatheads") you love to devour fakin' bacon, faux riblets, and dairy-free cheese, we'd say you've learned to fake it for animals quite well too. No small feat.

That's what we're helping you to achieve with this cookbook. Fake it until you make it, right? You may turn out to be an award-winning chef someday, but until you become a master of culinary arts, these recipes will get you through. To summarize: this cookbook will put Betty Crocker to shame and do so in a fraction of the time Ms. Crocker spent making her…uh…cheesecakes that are in the freezer section of the grocery store?

We've definitely had our share of culinary catastrophes over the years (we thought smoke alarms were meant to go off while you're making toast), so we wanted to let you lucky readers in on our tricks of the trade. And, no, we're not going to make you go searching for spelt flour or agar-agar. We'll keep things easy for ya.

VEGANS—WHAT *CAN* YOU EAT?

Back in the day, there was this stereotype that vegans only ate twigs or berries or lettuce or rocks or…well, you get the point. By the end of this cookbook, that stereotype will just be the punch line to a really bad joke. If you're wondering if vegans can eat this thing or that thing, ask yourself this simple question: Did it come from someone with a pulse? If the answer is yes, well then, it's not vegan. Hot dogs? Had a pulse. Chicken strips? Had a pulse. Glass of milk? Came from someone with a pulse. We have a problem with eating someone or something that came from someone who could stare back at us at one point (except for potatoes…mmm. Stare on, taters!).

Seriously, there's a vegan alternative for almost everything out there. The options available these days are amazing, and we fully recommend taking advantage of them. You can enjoy a veggie dog at a ballpark, throw some faux chicken patties on the grill at a BBQ, and grab a pint of your favorite dairy-free ice cream from your local grocery store. The possibilities are endless! Get started on your gluttonous cooking journey right now.

STOCK YOUR KITCHEN

Your local dollar store has lots of staples that'll help you get your kitchen necessities together on the cheap. So look under your bed or in the cushions of the communal couch for some spare change (you might want to wear gloves—you never know what you may find in there) and get the following for a buck each:

- Spices: salt, pepper, garlic salt/pepper, oregano/Italian seasoning, parsley, granulated onion, chili powder, seasoning salt, cinnamon, etc.
- Large dishes perfect for microwaving soups and pastas
- Storage containers
- Foil, plastic wrap, resealable bags, etc.
- Balsamic vinegar
- Olive oil
- Flatware and utensils
- Dish towels

- Oven mitts
- Canned goods: beans, veggies, tomatoes
- Pasta
- Salad dressing: A lot of Italian dressings are vegan!
- Ramen
- Tea
- Cereal (they usually have generic brands for Cheerios, Fruit Loops, and such)
- Salsa
- Rice
- Soy nuts
- Paper towels and napkins

The bottom line: Maybe you've been vegan for years, maybe you've just gone vegan, or maybe you're looking for a quick way to feed yourself or a reason to hit on the vegan in your psych class. Whatever your motive, we hope you'll enjoy this cookbook, It'll make your life just a bit simpler, so you can, you know, graduate from college and all that. We care about you, after all. We know, we know: we're so thoughtful. Compliment us later—now it's time to get your grub on!

VEGAN ALTERNATIVES TO MEATY, EGGY, AND MILKY STUFF

Here's an extensive list of all the vegan faux products you could ever want, as well as where you can find them. We've italicized all of our faves, so start with them. Once you think you can lose the training wheels, feel free to move on to the other awesome faux foods.

Note: Please check the ingredients of the items you buy to make sure they're vegan. Often, manufacturers put whey, milk fat, etc., in breads, cereals, and other products. For a list of ingredients you should look out for, please e-mail peta2@peta2.com.

vegan cheese

- *Galaxy Nutritional Foods:* Vegan Slices (American and Mozzarella), Vegan Grated Topping (Parmesan flavor), Vegan Blocks (Cheddar and Mozzarella), Rice Vegan Slices (American, Cheddar, Pepper Jack)

    galaxyfoods.com

- *Nutritional Yeast* (a delicious no-cow, low-cal cheese alternative): *Red Star*, Frontier Natural, KAL

  redstaryeast.com

  frontiercoop.com

- *Sheese:* Original Creamy, *Blue Style*, Cheddar Style with Chives, Cheshire Style, Edam Style, *Gouda Style*, Medium Cheddar Style, Mozzarella Style, Smoked Cheddar Style, *Strong Cheddar Style*, Garlic & Herb Creamy, and Mexican Style Creamy

  buteisland.com

- *Teese:* Mozzarella Vegan Cheese, Cheddar Vegan Cheese, and Nacho Vegan Cheese

  teesecheese.com

- *Tofutti:* American Soy-Cheese Slices and Mozzarella Soy-Cheese Slices

  tofutti.com

- *Vegan Gourmet: Cheddar Cheese Alternative, Mozzarella Cheese Alternative, Monterey Jack Cheese Alternative, and Nacho Cheese Alternative*

  imearthkind.com

vegan cream cheese

- *Tofutti: Better Than Cream Cheese:* Plain, *French Onion, Herbs & Chives*, Garlic & Herb, Garden Veggie, and Non-Hydrogenated Plain

  tofutti.com

- *Vegan Gourmet:* Cream cheese

  imearthkind.com

vegan egg alternatives

- *Ener-G Egg Replacer*

  ener-g.com

vegan margarine/butter

- *Earth Balance*

  earthbalancenatural.com

- *Willow Run*
- *Spectrum Naturals*

  spectrumorganics.com

vegan mayonnaise

- *Nayonaise:* Original, Fat-Free, and Dijon Style

  nasoya.com

- *Vegenaise: Original, Organic, Grapeseed Oil, and Expeller Pressed*

  imearthkind.com

- *Spectrum:* Light Canola Mayo, Eggless, Vegan

  spectrumorganics.com

vegan "meat"

- *Boca:* Chili, Original Boca Burger, *Vegan Burger*, Vegan Burger with Organic Soy, Chik'n Nuggets, Chik'n Patties, Spicy Chik'n Patties, and *Ground Crumbles*

  bocaburger.com

- *Dr. Praeger's:* Bombay Veggie Burgers, California Veggie Burgers, California Veggieballs, Italian Veggie Burgers, Tex Mex Veggie Burgers

  drpraegers.com

- *Field Roast Grain Meat Co.:* Roast Loaves in Lentil Sage, Wild Mushroom and Smoked Tomato, Celebration Roast, Deli Sliced in Lentil Sage, Deli Sliced in Wild Mushroom and Smoked Tomato, Sunflower Country-Style Cutlet, Hazelnut Herb Cutlet, Coconut Breaded Cutlet, Chipotle Corn Cutlet, Porcini Dijon Cutlet, Sausages in Italian, Mexican Chipotle, and Smoked Apple Sage, Classic Meatloaf, White Truffle Country Pate

  fieldroast.com

- *Gardein:* beef and chicken available through distributors throughout Canada and the United States, including Sysco, Neptune, and others.

  gardein.com

- *Gardenburger:* Veggie Medley Burger, Black Bean Chipotle Burger, Garden Vegan Burger, Flame Grilled Burger, The California Burger, Herb Crusted Cutlet, *BBQ Riblets*, Veggie Breakfast Sausage, Breaded Chik'n, Gourmet Hula

  gardenburger.com

- *Lightlife:* Smart Dogs, Tofu Pups, Smart Deli Pepperoni, Smart Deli Turkey, Smart Deli Ham, Smart Deli Bologna, Gimme Lean Sausage, Gimme Lean Beef, Smart Ground Original, Smart Ground Taco & Burrito, Smart Strips Chick'n, Smart Strips Steak, Light Burgers, Smart BBQ, Smart Tex Mex, Smart Chili, Orange Sesame Chick'n, Garlic Teriyaki Chick'n, Smart M'tballs, Smart Links Breakfast, Smart Bacon

  lightlife.com

- *Lumen/Stonewall's:* Original Mild Jerquee, BBQ "Beef"

Jerquee, Teriyaki "Beef" Jerquee, Tandoori "Chicken" Jerquee, Original Wild Jerquee, Spicy "Chicken" Jerquee, Peppy "Pepperoni" Jerquee, Hot "Pastrami" Jerquee, Cajun "Bacon" Jerquee

> *soybean.com*

- *May Wah: Vegetarian Chicken Steak, Vegetarian S.W. Ham*, Vegan Stewed Ham, Vegan Smoked Ham, Vegetarian Chicken G Nuggets, Vegetarian Meat Steak with Pepper, Vegetarian Roasted Salted Chicken, Vegetarian Codfish Ball, Vegetarian Shrimp Ball, Vegetarian String Meat Ball, Vegetarian Chicken Leg, Vegetarian Chicken Ball, Vegetarian Beef Chunks, Vegetarian Prawns, Vegetarian Fish Nuggets/Fingers, Vegetarian Beef Ball, Vegetarian Frozen Q Tofu, Vegetarian Smoked Ham, Vegetarian Bacon Ham, Vegetarian Chicken Ham, Vegetarian Tuna, Vegetarian Sweet & Sour Soybean, Vegetarian Prepared Mushroom, Vegetarian Mushroom Seaweed Ball, Vegetarian Seaweed Nuggets, Vegetarian Squid, Vegetarian Crispy Meat Ball, Vegetarian Beef Burger, Vegetarian Bar-B-Q Sauce Gizzard, Vegetarian Abalone, Vegetarian Fish, Vegetarian Grilled Eel, Vegetarian Cocktail Sausage, Vegetarian Salmon, *Vegetarian Citrus Spare Ribs*, Vegetarian Chicken Roll, Vegetarian Black Pepper Steak, Vegetarian Fish Ham, Vegetarian Chicken Bites, *Vegetarian Goong Bao Chicken*, Vegetarian BBQ Pork, *Vegetarian Golden Fish Fillet*, Vegetarian Chicken Ball, Vegetarian Salty Salmon-Slice, Vegetarian Black Pepper Steak, Vegetarian Smoked Turkey, Vegetarian Soybean Fluff (fridge), Vegetarian

Pepper Steak, Vegetarian Healthy Chicken, Vegetarian Smoked Chicken, Vegetarian Squid Rolls, Vegetarian Hot Pot Ingredients, Fried Bean Curd with Agar-Agar, Vegetarian Lotus Seeds Chicken, Vegetarian Fried Soybean Slice, Vegetarian Crab Roll, Vegetarian Duck Meat, Vegetarian Toast Ham, Vegetarian Flavor Noodle, Vegetarian Seaweed Strips, Vegetarian Shrimp Balls and Prawns, Vegetarian Abalone Slice, Vegetarian Kidney

vegieworld.com

- **Morningstar Farms:** *Veggie Steak Strips*, Sausage Style Recipe Crumbles, *Chik'n Strips*, Grillers Recipe Crumbles, Vegan Veggie Burgers

    seeveggiesdifferently.com

- **Tofurky:** Roast, Franks, Foot-Long Franks, Chipotle Franks, Breakfast Links, Original Deli Slices, *Peppered Deli Slices*, *Hickory Smoked Deli Slices*, Cranberry & Stuffing Deli Slices, Italian Deli Slices, "Philly Style" Steak Deli Slices, *Beerbrats*, Sweet Italian Sausage, *Kielbasa*, Original SuperBurgers, TexMex SuperBurgers, Five Grain Tempeh, Soy Tempeh, Spicy Veggie Tempeh, Original Jurky, Peppered Jurky

    tofurky.com

- **Worthington Foods:** *Chic-ketts*, Choplets, Chili, Big Franks, Dinner Cuts, Protein Links, Little Links, Low-Fat Big Franks, Redi-Burger Patties, Tender Bits, Vege-Burger Patties, Low-Fat Vegetable Steaks, Multi-Grain Cutlets, Vegetable Skallops

    worthingtonfoods.com

- **Yves:** Hot Dogs, Brats, Beef Skewers, Chicken Skewers,

Meatless Bologna, Meatless Ham, Meatless Turkey, Meatless Salami, Meatless Pepperoni, Roast Without Beef, Meatless Smoked Chicken, Chicken Burger, Beef Burger, Canadian Bacon, Breakfast Patties, Chili, Lasagna, Penne, Santa Fe Meatless Beef, Thai Lemongrass Meatless Chicken, Ground Round Original, Ground Taco Stuffers, Ground Turkey, Asian Ground Round Lettuce Wraps

yvesveggie.com

vegan milk alternatives

- *Almond Breeze:* Original, Vanilla, Chocolate Almond Milk

  bluediamond.com

- *Almond Dream:* Original and unsweetened

  tastethedream.com

- *Rice Dream:* Carob, Enriched Chocolate, Enriched Original, Enriched Vanilla, Heartwise Original, Heartwise Vanilla, Horchata, Original, Supreme Chocolate Chai, Supreme Vanilla Hazelnut, Vanilla

  tastethedream.com

- *Ryza:* Original, Vanilla

  ryza.ca

- *Silk:* Organic Plain, Vanilla, Unsweetened, Natural Plain, Very Vanilla, Chocolate, Light Plain, Nog

  silksoymilk.com

- *Edensoy:* Organic Carob, Chocolate, Extra Original, Extra Vanilla, Light Original, Vanilla, Oriental, Unsweetened

  edenfoods.com

- *8th Continent:* Original Vanilla, Chocolate, Light Original, Vanilla, Fat-Free Vanilla, Original

    8thcontinent.com

- *Soy Dream:* Classic Vanilla, Enriched Chocolate, Enriched original, Enriched Vanilla

    tastethedream.com

- *Natura:* Original, Vanilla, Strawberry, Chocolate, Unsweetened, Light Original

    nutrisoya.com

- *Vitasoy:* Creamy original, Smooth Vanilla, Rich Chocolate

    vitasoy-usa.com

- *Westsoy:* Plus Plain, Vanilla, Low-Fat Plain, Light Plain, Nonfat Plain

    westsoy.biz

vegan sour cream

- *Tofutti:* Plain Sour Supreme, Guacamole Sour Supreme, *Non-Hydrogenated Sour Supreme*

    tofutti.com

- *Vegan Gourmet:* Sour Cream

    imearthkind.com

PART TWO

RECIPES YOU'LL LOVE

BREAKFAST

You know what they say: Breakfast is the most important meal of the day. Hell, yeah! How else are you going to motivate yourself to stop hitting the snooze button and get moving for those early classes? And forget those grease-laden breakfasts that just make you more tired. These recipes will keep your energized and full, at least until the dining hall opens for lunch. There's nothing more embarrassing than hearing your stomach growl echo throughout a lecture hall, but don't worry; we've got you covered. The best thing about these recipes is that you can enjoy them whenever you're in need of a little breakfasty goodness—whether the sun's just coming up or about to go down.

DID YOU KNOW?

Eggs are horrible for your health. A single egg has as much cholesterol as three servings of beef tenderloin. (All vegan foods are cholesterol-free.) Many grocery-store eggs are infected with salmonella, a dangerous type of bacteria that causes diarrhea and fever in humans. Yuck.

BREAKFAST/DESSERT PARFAIT

Perfect for those days when you can't tell where last night ended and today began.

1/2 cup granola

1 (6-ounce) container vegan yogurt (vanilla or fruit-flavored)

1 banana, sliced

1/4 cup sliced strawberries or raspberries

In a tall glass, layer all the ingredients, sand-art style.

Makes 1 serving.

MEDITERRANEAN MUESLI

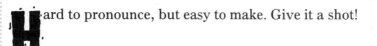

Hard to pronounce, but easy to make. Give it a shot!

- 1 cup rolled oats
- 1 cup vanilla soy milk or rice milk
- 1 cup plain vegan yogurt
- 3 tablespoons chopped dried apricots
- 3 tablespoons chopped dates

Mix all the ingredients together in a large bowl and refrigerate for 2 hours. Top with your fave type of berries.

Makes 1 serving.

"I'M, LIKE, SO EASY!" BLUEBERRY PANCAKES

Easier than dozing off in bio-chem, these tasty babies can be made in a mug, cup bowl, or whatever you have lying around. (Umm, maybe it's time to clean your room. Ew.)

2 cups Bisquick (or any other vegan pancake mix)

1 cup soy milk

3 teaspoons egg replacer mixed with 4 tablespoons water

1/2 cup frozen blueberries

Maple syrup, to taste (optional)

Powdered sugar, to taste (optional)

Vegan margarine, to taste (optional)

Mix the first four ingredients together. Pour evenly into two mugs and microwave each for 1 or 2 minutes, until completely cooked. Add maple syrup, powdered sugar, and margarine. Voila!

Makes 2 servings.

MORNING IN MEXICO SCRAMBLE

All the great tastes of Mexico in one bite: fun and spicy, like Cabo, and a little rough around the edges, like Tijuana.

1 (16-ounce) package firm tofu, drained and rinsed

2 cups corn tortilla chips

1 teaspoon onion powder

2 cups salsa

Mash tofu and microwave for 4 minutes. Add tortilla chips and onion powder and stir to blend in with tofu. (You can break the chips up a little, if you want.) Cook for about 2 minutes and stir. Add salsa and nuke for another minute, until chips start to soften and salsa is heated through.

Makes 3 servings.

TOO-LATE-TO-GO-TO-THE-DINING-HALL TOFU MASH

Missed the breakfast hours at the dining hall? Never fear —tofu is here!

- 1 (16-ounce) package extra-firm tofu, drained and crumbled
- 1 slice vegan cheese
- 1 (7-ounce) can chopped tomatoes, drained
- 1 tablespoon mustard
- 2 teaspoons soy sauce
- Salt and pepper, to taste

Mix everything together and nuke for 2 minutes.

Makes 3 servings.

FRESHMAN FRITTATA

So easy, a freshman could make it! Just kidding…

2 cups frozen hash-
brown potatoes

1/2 cup shredded carrot
(can be bought pre-
shredded)

1 teaspoon onion powder

2 tablespoons vegan
margarine

Salt and pepper, to taste

1/4 cup egg replacer
mixed with 1 cup
water

1/2 cup soy milk

1 teaspoon mustard

1 dash hot sauce

1 cup vegan bacon bits

1/2 cup shredded vegan
cheddar cheese

In a large bowl, mix together the hash browns, carrots, onion powder, and margarine. Cover and nuke for 5 minutes, stirring once or twice. Season with salt and pepper. In another bowl, mix together the egg replacer, soy milk, mustard, and hot sauce. Stir in the bacon bits and pour the egg-replacer mixture over the hash-brown mixture. Stir everything together. Cover and nuke for 3 minutes. Give it a good stir, then nuke for another 5 minutes. If your microwave does not have a turntable, rotate the dish two or three times during the cooking process. Sprinkle the cheese on top, cover, and microwave for another minute, or until the cheese has melted.

Makes 2 servings.

FRUIT SKEWER WITH "YOGURT" SAUCE

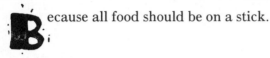ecause all food should be on a stick.

- 1/2 cup strawberry vegan yogurt
- 1 teaspoon agave nectar (you can find it at your local grocery store, next to the honey)
- 1/4 teaspoon grated nutmeg
- 2 teaspoons lemon juice (you can buy a squirt bottle of lemon juice to use instead of fresh, if it's easier—it certainly keeps better!)
- 1 (16-ounce) plastic tub of pre-cut fruit of your choice
- 4 wooden skewers

Combine the yogurt, agave nectar, nutmeg, and lemon juice. Set aside. Thread the fruit on the skewers. Serve with the yogurt sauce for dipping.

Makes 1 serving.

GREEK NOMELETTE

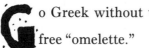o Greek without the hazing (or the yolks) with our egg-free "omelette."

- 1 cup vegan pancake mix
- 1/2 cup soy milk
- 1 1/2 teaspoons egg replacer mixed with 2 tablespoons water
- 1/4 cup tofu, drained and cubed
- 8–10 kalamata olives, pitted
- 1/4 cup frozen spinach, thawed
- 1 teaspoon garlic powder

In a small bowl, mix together the pancake mix, soy milk, and egg replacer/water mixture. Stir until blended. Add the tofu, olives, spinach, and garlic powder. Microwave for 2 minutes, or until solid.

Makes 1 serving.

TOASTY SAUSAGE SURPRISE

The surprise? Your omni friends will never know this isn't real sausage.

1 (14-ounce) tube veggie sausage, crumbled

2 cups soy milk

2 tablespoons vegan margarine

Salt and pepper, to taste

1/4 cup flour

6 slices of bread, toasted

Mix together the sausage, soy milk, margarine, and salt and pepper in a bowl. Heat for 3 minutes, then add a dash of flour while stirring. Heat for an additional 2 minutes. Repeat this flour-adding process until the mixture is thick. Place toast on plates and top with the sausage mixture.

Makes 3 servings.

CRUMB BUM BREAKFAST COBBLER

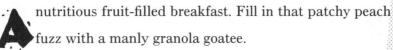

A nutritious fruit-filled breakfast. Fill in that patchy peach fuzz with a manly granola goatee.

1 (16-ounce) can sliced peaches, drained

1 (15-ounce) can pear halves, drained and sliced

1/3 cup orange juice (optional)

1 1/2 cups low-fat granola cereal

Place the peaches, pears, and orange juice in a bowl. Top with the granola. Nuke for 5 minutes, then remove from the microwave and let stand for 2 minutes before serving.

Makes 4 servings.

THE MORNING-AFTER SCRAMBLE

After you're done scrambling to figure out what, exactly, *in the hell you did last night,* whip up a batch of this eggless scramble, sit down, and try to remember where you were and why you're missing a shoe.

8 ounces salsa

1 (16-ounce) package extra-firm tofu, mashed

Salt, pepper, and garlic powder, to taste

1/3 cup soy milk

1/4 cup nutritional yeast

Drain most of the liquid from the salsa, mix in a bowl with the tofu, and nuke for about 1 minute, or until heated through. Add salt, pepper, and garlic powder. Mix the soy milk and nutritional yeast together in a cup until thick and creamy, then add to the tofu mixture. Nuke for about 2 minutes or until hot, stopping and stirring halfway through. Eat with toast, potatoes, or a faux meat of some kind.

Makes 1 serving.

BUTT UGLY STICKY BUNS

When plated, they look like a bunch of muddy guys mooning you, but try not to let that turn you off. They're delicious, we promise.

1/3 cup firmly packed dark brown sugar

3 tablespoons vegan margarine

1 tablespoon water

1/3 cup chopped nuts (optional)

1 (8-ounce) can refrigerated vegan biscuits

Combine the brown sugar, margarine, and water in an 8-inch round microwave-safe dish. Nuke, uncovered, for 2 minutes, or until the margarine melts. Stir, then spread evenly across the bottom of the dish, covering the entire surface. Sprinkle with nuts (if you are using them), and then place the biscuits on top. Nuke on medium heat for 4 to 5 minutes, or until the biscuits are firm and no longer doughy. Let stand for 2 minutes and then dump onto a plate, upside down.

Makes 4 servings.

NOT-JUST-FOR-HIPPIES GRANOLA

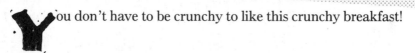

You don't have to be crunchy to like this crunchy breakfast!

1/2 cup vegan granola

3 tablespoons raisins or chopped dates (optional)

1 tablespoon almonds or nut of choice (optional)

1 (6-ounce) container soy yogurt (your fave flavor)

Mix everything together and eat.

Makes 1 serving.

BRAINY BAC'N CHEESE TOAST

Start your morning—okay, afternoon—off right with a gooey breakfast that'll keep you going through that 3 o'clock class.

- 2 slices bread, toasted
- 8 cherry tomatoes, halved
- 4 tablespoons vegan bacon bits
- 2 slices vegan cheddar cheese

Top one slice of bread with tomatoes, bacon bits, and cheese. Microwave for 2 minutes or until cheese is melted, and top with the remaining slice of bread.

Makes 1 serving.

HANGOVER HELPER

Once you can stand to see the light in the refrigerator, start undoing last night's damage by munching on this yummy breakfast bagel.

2 tablespoons vegan mayonnaise

Salt, pepper, and onion powder, to taste

8 vegan chicken strips, thawed

2 slices vegan cheese

1 bagel, sliced in half

Mix the mayo with a little salt, pepper, and onion powder and set aside. Put the chicken strips on a plate, top with the cheese slices, and nuke for 1 minute. Meanwhile, toast the bagel. Spread the seasoned mayo on both halves of the bagel and place the chicken on one half. Put bagel halves together and eat.

Makes 1 serving.

SUNDAY MORNING "SAUSAGE" IN A BLANKET

When Saturday night has left you semi-conscious, barely a biped and unable to even use a can opener, quietly put together these easy ingredients, eat, enjoy, and then crawl back under the covers.

2 vegan sausages
1 (8-ounce) can vegan crescent rolls

Cut each sausage in half, and then cut each half lengthwise. Wrap the crescent dough around each piece. Pop in the microwave for 10 minutes or until the dough is fluffy.

Makes 2 servings.

BROKE-ASS CINNAMON ROLLS

Flat broke? Make your dough go further with this cheap and tasty pastry.

1 slice white bread

Vegan margarine, to taste

Cinnamon, to taste

Sugar, to taste

Cut the crust off the bread. Flatten the bread with a can or a rolling pin and spread it with the margarine. Sprinkle with cinnamon and sugar. Roll up like a burrito and cut into mini-rolls (or just leave it as a burrito, if that sounds good or you're in a hurry). Microwave for 15 seconds, or until margarine is melted.

Makes 1 serving.

BOOTY SHAKIN' BAGEL

There is nothing better than a bagel—especially after a long night of dancin'!

2 tablespoons vegan cream cheese
2 tablespoons jelly (your fave flavor)
1 bagel, sliced in half

Spread the cream cheese on half the bagel and the jam on the other half. Smoosh together and eat.

Makes 1 serving.

NO-NEED-TO-VISIT-A-DINER-FOR-HASH-BROWNS CASSEROLE

As fun as it is to walk two miles to suck down some weak coffee and scarf some greasy potatoes, this dish requires a lot less effort and tastes better too.

1/2 cup nutritional yeast

1/2 cup soy milk

1 tablespoon olive oil

1 teaspoon garlic powder

Salt and pepper, to taste

Olive oil, for coating

1 (20-ounce) bag shredded potatoes (can also use hash-brown-style potatoes), thawed

1 (12-ounce) bag veggie burger crumbles, thawed

1 (10-ounce) bag frozen broccoli florets, thawed

Hot sauce (optional)

Mix the nutritional yeast, soy milk, olive oil, garlic powder, salt, and pepper together to create the cheesy sauce. Set aside. Take a microwave-safe container, lightly coat it with olive oil, and layer the potatoes on the bottom. Then, add the crumbles and top with the broccoli, cheese sauce, and hot sauce, if using. Microwave on high for 5 minutes or until everything is hot.

Makes 4 servings.

SANDWICHES

Sandwiches are the most amazing food in the world. That's a fact, not opinion: seriously, who doesn't like sandwiches? They're customizable, portable, filling, and yummy—not to mention easy to make. Whether you like to pile on the fake meat, load up on veggies, smother your bread with hummus, or tackle all three at once, we've got the sandwich for you. And if you want to make one for us while you're at it, well, let's just say we wouldn't hate you for it.

DID YOU KNOW?

Fruits and vegetables, also known as "plant foods," have been shown to have "chemopreventive" properties. The risk of lung cancer in heavy smokers has been shown to be reduced in populations that eat generous amounts of plant foods.

GREEK WEEK PITA

A safe and tasty alternative to chugging beer from the top of a human pyramid.

3 ounces vegan cream cheese, softened to room
    temperature

1 tablespoon vegan sour cream

1/2 teaspoon dried parsley (optional)

1 pita, sliced in half

1–2 leaves lettuce

2–3 cherry tomatoes, halved

Chopped black olives, to taste

Mix together the cream cheese, sour cream, and optional parsley. Stuff into each side of the pita, then add the rest of the ingredients to the pita.

Makes 1 serving.

SLOPPY JOELS

Just as "meaty" as the original Joes, except…well, there's no meat.

- 1 (15.5-ounce) can sloppy joe sauce (Manwich brand is vegan; watch out for anchovies in the Worcestershire sauce in some brands)
- 1 (12-ounce) bag veggie burger crumbles
- 4 buns
- Pickle slices (optional)

Combine the sauce and crumbles in a microwave-safe bowl. Nuke for 2 minutes, or until hot. Place on the buns along with pickle slices (if you like pickles), and serve.

Makes 4 servings.

LATE-NIGHT SLOPPY MOES

It's been a long day, and you've got at least another hour's worth of studying ahead. Take a short break and get a little messy—you deserve it.

1 1/2 cups veggie burger crumbles

1 teaspoon onion powder

2 1/2 cups tomato puree

Pepper, to taste

1 tablespoon soy sauce

1 1/2 tablespoons mustard

1 tablespoon sugar

1 (4-ounce) can green chiles

4 buns

Nuke the crumbles in a bowl until warm. Mix in the rest of the ingredients (except the buns) and heat for 3 minutes. Scoop onto the buns and eat.

Makes 4 servings.

UPPER-CRUST FINGER SANDWICHES

When the family visits, serve 'em these sandwiches. They'll be so impressed by how well you're getting along on your own. Your 'rents might even overlook that towering heap of dirty clothes in the corner.

3 (8-ounce) containers vegan cream cheese, softened

1 tablespoon chives

1 (4-ounce) jar sliced green olives, drained

2 tablespoon Dijon mustard

2 loaves sliced, firm bread (white, wheat, rye, or pumpernickel work best)

1 trip to your local salad bar to pick up a cup of sliced cucumbers

1 (5.5-ounce) package faux lunch meat slices (try faux salami, pepperoni, or ham)

To make three different sandwich fillings, mix one container of cream cheese with the chives, mix another with the olives, and mix the third with the mustard, all in separate bowls. To make cucumber sandwiches, spread a thin layer of the cream cheese and chive mixture onto a slice of bread and top with cucumber slices. To make olive sandwiches, spread the cream cheese and olive mixture onto a slice of bread. To make meat sandwiches, spread a thin layer of the cream cheese and mustard mixture onto a slice of bread and top with a slice of lunch meat. Top each sandwich with another slice of bread and cut each sandwich into quarters. Pile the finger sandwiches onto a plate, cover with plastic wrap, and chill in the fridge briefly before serving.

Makes 8 servings.

CHICK-UN PARM SAMMICH

Warning: Sammich may spontaneously disappear if left unattended with roommate.

- 1 vegan chicken patty
- 2 slices whole-wheat bread
- 2 tablespoons marinara sauce
- 1 slice vegan mozzarella cheese

Microwave the chicken patty according to directions on the box. Then microwave the marinara sauce for 30 seconds, or until warm. Place the chicken patty on one slice of bread and top with the marinara sauce and cheese. Add the other slice of bread and eat.

Makes 1 serving.

NOTE:

If you're making this to-go, wrap it up in foil. It will keep the sammich warm until you're ready to eat!

HEARTY HUMMUS SANDWICH

A hearty, rustic sandwich fit for a king—or the captain of the football team.

Hummus, to taste

2 slices thick-crusted sourdough bread

1–2 leaves lettuce

3–4 cherry tomatoes, halved

Spread the desired amount of hummus on both slices of the bread. Place the lettuce and tomatoes on one piece of the bread, then top with the other piece.

Makes 1 serving.

CRAM SANDWICH

Stuff this tasty sandwich in your cake hole so you can go back to stuffing your brain with useless facts and figures.

2 tablespoons vegan mayonnaise

3 slices vegan whole-wheat bread, toasted

6 slices vegan turkey deli slices

6–8 cherry tomatoes, halved

2 tablespoons vegan bacon bits

2 large lettuce leaves

Spread mayo on one side of each slice of toast. Place one slice on a plate, mayo side up, and top with half of the turkey, cherry tomatoes, bacon bits, and lettuce. Add another slice of bread, mayo side up, and top with the remaining turkey, tomatoes, bacon bits, and lettuce. Add the third slice of bread, mayo side down this time, and squish the sandwich down so you can eat it!

Makes 1 serving.

SALAD-BAGEL

Who says eating bagels will make your middle look like a doughnut? This healthy bagel sandwich has more foliage in it than the school's greenhouse.

Vegan margarine, to taste

1 sesame bagel, sliced in half

Your favorite veggies from the local salad bar

1 tablespoon zesty Italian salad dressing

1/4 cup shredded vegan mozzarella cheese

Spread margarine on the bagel halves and set aside. Toss the veggies in a bowl, add the salad dressing, and mix thoroughly. Scoop the mixture onto one bagel slice, sprinkle with the cheese, and top with the other half of the bagel.

Makes 1 serving.

ASPARA–STUFFED PARM SANDWICH

The fanciest thing you'll ever brown bag to lunch, this savory and satisfying sandwich is guaranteed to get rid of those work-study-slave-wage-job blues in just one bite.

1 (10-ounce) package frozen cut asparagus

2 slices bread

1/2 teaspoon vegan margarine

2 tablespoons vegan mayonnaise

2 teaspoons nutritional yeast

Pepper, to taste

1–2 leaves lettuce

Nuke the asparagus until warm, 2 to 3 minutes. Spread one side of each bread slice with 1/4 teaspoon margarine and 1 table-spoon mayonnaise. Add some asparagus and sprinkle with nutritional yeast and pepper. Add lettuce and smoosh the two pieces of bread together.

Makes 1 serving.

GPA BOOSTER

They say veggies are brain food. Well, if that's true, this tasty wrap will help you pass chemistry faster than hooking up with your TA.

2 tablespoons hummus

1 (10-inch) flour tortilla

1/4 cup shredded lettuce

1 tablespoon alfalfa sprouts

3–4 cherry tomatoes, halved

Diced cucumbers, to taste (go to your local salad bar and grab them pre-cut)

Salt and pepper, to taste

Spread the hummus on the tortilla. Dump the remaining ingredients onto the wrap, roll up like a burrito, and enjoy!

Makes 1 serving.

MEATBALL ANTI-HERO

Just like the one you used to get at your local sub shop, but rest assured: there's no mystery meat in this hearty version.

4 vegan meatless meatballs, frozen

2 tablespoons spaghetti sauce

1 hoagie roll, split lengthwise

2 slices vegan mozzarella cheese

Place the meatballs in a microwave-safe dish and heat until hot, about 45 seconds. Remove from the microwave, add the spaghetti sauce, cover, and return to the microwave. Heat for another 2 minutes, or until bubbly. Spoon the meatballs and sauce onto the bread and top with the cheese. Microwave until the cheese melts, about 30 seconds.

Makes 1 serving.

NOTE:

If you have a toaster oven, you can skip the microwave and toast the whole mess until the cheese is melted.

TOKEN BOCA LT

You didn't think we'd make a vegan cookbook without throwing at least one veggie burger recipe in here, did you?

1 Boca burger

2 slices whole-wheat bread

Vegan mayo, to taste

Ketchup, to taste

Few pieces lettuce

4 cherry tomatoes, halved

Heat the Boca burger in the microwave according to the directions on the box, and toast the bread. Spread mayo and ketchup on one slice of bread, add lettuce and tomato, and top with the burger and other slice of bread.

Makes 1 serving.

TAILGATIN' TOFU REUBEN

Have you been tailgating lately? Uh huh…break out the 'body paint and show 'em what you're made of with this stackable (shirts optional) sandwich.

1 (16-ounce) package extra-firm tofu, drained and squeezed
    to remove excess water (reserve the water)
Sauerkraut, to taste
Nutritional yeast, to taste
Mustard, to taste
2 slices rye bread, toasted

Cut a couple of very thin slices off the block of tofu. Set aside. (Place the remaining tofu back in the water, and save and refrigerate for another recipe.) Spread some mustard on one of the pieces of toast and top with the tofu slices. Add some saucrkraut and sprinkle with nutritional yeast. Top with the other piece of toast and eat.

Makes 1 serving.

SHAM AND CHEEZ

Make your classmates jealous as you roll into class, home-made sham-and-cheez deliciousness in hand. You'll have them drooling over vegan food in no time!

1 cup vegan pancake mix

1/2 cup soy milk

1 1/2 teaspoons egg replacer mixed with 2 tablespoons water

4 slices vegan ham, torn into pieces

1/2 cup shredded vegan cheese

Mustard, for dipping

In a small bowl, mix together the pancake mix, soy milk, and egg replacer/water mixture. Stir until blended. Add the ham and cheese. Microwave for 2 minutes, or until solid. Pry out of the bowl and dip into mustard.

Makes 1 serving.

THE HANGOVER "HAM"WICH

Figure out where you're at, find your way home, vow to never drink again, fix this easy breakfast for a late lunch, have a drink. Repeat.

4 slices vegan ham

2 slices vegan cheese

1 pita, sliced in half

Stuff the ham and cheese in the pita and nuke for 45 seconds.

Makes 1 serving.

"DON'T BE A CHUMP" CHICKPEA SANDWICH

eriously. You heard us.

1/2 (15-ounce) can of chickpeas, mashed with a fork

Italian dressing, to taste

2 slices bread

1/4 cup shredded carrots

4 cherry tomatoes, halved

Mix the chickpeas with some Italian dressing and spread on one slice of bread. Top with the shredded carrots, the tomatoes, and add the other slice of bread.

Makes 1 serving.

POULTRYGEIST PITA

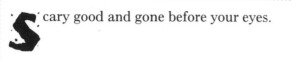

Scary good and gone before your eyes.

8 vegan chicken strips, heated in the microwave for 1
    minute (or until heated through)

1 (15-ounce) can mixed vegetables, drained

2 tablespoons vegan mayonnaise

Salt and pepper, to taste

1 pita, sliced in half

1–2 leaves lettuce

Tear the chicken strips into pieces. Put in a bowl and add the veggies, mayo, salt, and pepper. Stir together. Stuff in the pita along with some lettuce.

Makes 1 serving.

HOLY 'MOLE SANDWICH

Whoever said condiment sandwiches aren't food clearly never had this guac masterpiece.

- 2 tablespoons store-bought guacamole (or use our recipe listed on page 218)
- 2 slices whole-wheat bread
- 2 cherry tomatoes, halved
- 1/4 cup shredded lettuce

Spread the guac on one of the slices of bread. Top with the lettuce and the tomatoes. Place the other slice of bread on top and eat.

Makes 1 serving.

LAZY PERSON'S GRILLED CHEEZE

It's 3 a.m. the night before your history final and you are starving. Lazy Person's Grilled Cheeze to the rescue!

2 slices vegan cheese
2 slices bread, toasted
Pickle slices (optional)

Place the slices of cheese between the two slices of bread. Put on a plate and toss in the microwave. Heat on high for 30 seconds, or until the cheese is melted. Open the sandwich and insert the pickle slices, if using. Close the sandwich and chow down.

Makes 1 serving.

RACHEL

Did you know that a vegetarian Reuben sandwich is sometimes called a "Rachel?" It's true—Wikipedia says so. Come on, don't act like you didn't use Wikipedia to write your entire research paper last week.

4 slices vegan bacon

2 slices vegan whole-wheat rye bread, toasted

2 slices vegan cheese

1/4 cup drained sauerkraut

2 tablespoons your favorite vegan salad dressing

Microwave the bacon according to the package instructions, or until hot. Place on the bread and top with the cheese. Nuke until the cheese is melted. Top with the kraut, dressing, and the other slice of bread and enjoy!

Makes 1 serving.

FAKE CHEEZ STEAK

This yummy, animal-friendly cheez steak is as fake as that quote you fudged for your English paper last week, but the deliciousness is oh-so-real!

1 tablespoon vegan mayonnaise

1 hoagie roll

1/2 (8-ounce) package vegan steak strips

3 slices vegan cheese

Salt and pepper, to taste

Spread the mayonnaise on the roll and set aside. Top the steak strips with the cheese and heat in the microwave until the cheese is melted, about 1 minute. Place on the roll. Sprinkle with salt and pepper and eat.

Makes 1 serving.

NOTE:

If you have a toaster oven, you can skip the microwave and toast the whole mess until the cheese is melted.

TOFU, OR NOT TOFU, THAT IS THE SANDWICH

Hey, Shakespeare, take a break from pondering existential dilemmas with this yummy sammie that would make even good ol' Will's heart beat in iambic pentameter.

8 ounces tofu, mashed

2 teaspoons onion powder

1 tablespoon roasted sunflower seeds

1 tablespoon vegan mayonnaise

1 tablespoon relish

2 teaspoons mustard

2 teaspoons soy sauce

1/4 teaspoon garlic powder

4 slices toast

2 leaves lettuce

4 cherry tomatoes, halved

Mix the tofu, onion powder, sunflower seeds, mayonnaise, relish, mustard, soy sauce, and garlic powder in a bowl. Spread onto two pieces of toast. Top each with a lettuce leaf and 4 tomato halves, and put remaining bread on top.

Makes 2 servings.

SCUZZ-FREE BBQ TOFU

When everything else in your fridge is furry, you can always depend on that block o' tofu to be as fresh as the day you bought it last summer. Seriously, your student I.D. will expire before that tofu, so enjoy a BBQ sandwich or two and then clean out your fridge.

1 (16-ounce) package extra-firm tofu, drained and cut in half horizontally

1 cup bottled BBQ sauce

4 sandwich rolls

Sandwich fixings (lettuce, tomato, etc.)

Wrap the tofu slices in paper towels and put on a plate. Top with another plate and place a heavy book on top. Refrigerate for an hour or so. Unwrap the tofu, pat dry, and place in a large bowl. Spoon ¾ cup of BBQ sauce over the tofu, cover the bowl, and let marinate overnight. The next day, place the tofu on a plate and nuke for 2 minutes. Cut the tofu into thin slices and place on sandwich rolls with the rest of your sandwich fixings. Spoon barbecue sauce over the sandwich fixings.

Makes 4 servings.

SPOTLIGHT ON: PEANUT BUTTER

Peanut butter is an extremely versatile food—after all, there aren't many foods you can use in a sandwich *and* a dessert. Well, we guess you *could* use hummus in a sandwich and a dessert, but we don't recommend it. Peanut butter is a protein-packed, stick-to-the-roof-of-your-mouth, delicious culinary device that we're sure you will love as much as we do. We apologize in advance if you become addicted.

DID YOU KNOW?

Healthy sources for protein include whole-wheat bread, oatmeal, beans, peanuts, peas, nuts, mushrooms, and broccoli. Too much protein, especially animal protein, can cause people to excrete calcium through their urine and increase their risk of osteoporosis. Too much protein can also strain the kidneys, leading to kidney disease. Vegans do not need to combine foods at each meal in order to be sure they're getting "complete protein." Grains, legumes, vegetables, nuts, and seeds provide all the essential amino acids.

KNOCK-OATS

Packed with peanutty protein and potassium, this breakfast of champions is a one-two punch of health and deliciousness.

1 package instant vegan oatmeal

1 banana, sliced thin

2 tablespoons peanut butter

1 teaspoon cinnamon

Prepare the oatmeal according to the package instructions. While hot, stir in the banana slices, peanut butter, and cinnamon.

Makes 1 serving.

WICKED GOOD WAFFLEWICH

Usually when someone is described as sweet, it means that they're ugly. No difference here. Super sweet, this wicked weird-looking PB-and-chocolate-chip monstrosity is fugly but fabulous.

2 vegan waffles, toasted

Vegan chocolate chips, to taste

Peanut butter, to taste

Maple syrup, to taste

Smear peanut butter on both waffles and then sprinkle them with the desired amount of chocolate chips. Nuke for about 10 seconds. Smash the waffles together and top it all off with some maple syrup.

Makes 1 serving.

ONE-HANDED BREAKFAST WRAP

A one-handed breakfast leaves the other hand free to hold your BlackBerry, iPod, or other stuff you might be carrying on your way to class.

2 tablespoons crunchy peanut butter

1 (10-inch) whole-grain flour tortilla

1 banana, sliced

1/2 apple, thinly sliced

2 tablespoons raisins

Spread the peanut butter on the tortilla. Layer the remaining ingredients on top. Roll tightly and eat.

Makes 1 serving.

PORTABLE PB&J

With this drip-resistant PB&J, you won't have to take valuable time away from ~~stalking people online~~ writing your English paper to eat.

Pita, split in half

3 tablespoons peanut butter

3 tablespoons strawberry jam

1 banana, sliced

Spread the inside of the pita halves with the peanut butter and jam. Stuff with the banana slices and eat.

Makes 1 serving.

PB AND BANANA SAMMIE

Decadent and filling, this is the reason Elvis kept splitting his jumpsuits.

2 tablespoons peanut butter

2 slices bread, toasted

1 banana, sliced

Spread the peanut butter on one slice of the bread. Put banana slices on top and cover with the other slice of bread.

Makes 1 serving.

THE NUT JOB SALAD

A crazy combo of nutty ingredients: This salad is more mixed-up than your ex, but a lot healthier for you.

1 cup Italian dressing

1/4 cup peanut butter (creamy or chunky)

1 (16-ounce) bag lettuce

Croutons, to taste (page 250)

Sunflower seeds or chopped peanuts, to taste

In a small bowl, gradually stir the dressing into the peanut butter. Toss the lettuce, croutons, and sunflower seeds or peanuts together in another bowl to make the salad. Place the salad in individual bowls and top with peanut butter dressing.

Makes 2 servings.

SUPER QUICKIE PEANUT SAUCE

Like most things this good, no matter how hard you try to make it last, you're done way too soon.

3 tablespoons peanut butter

5 tablespoons hot water

2 teaspoons lemon juice

2 tablespoons soy sauce

1 teaspoon chili-garlic sauce

Combine the peanut butter, water, lemon juice, soy sauce, and chili-garlic sauce in a medium-sized bowl and stir until combined. (Add more water if you want a thinner consistency.) Nuke for 30 seconds. Serve over steamed veggies and fried or steamed tofu, or use as a dipping sauce for veggies and tofu.

Makes 2 servings.

BUNNY BUTTER SPREAD

Rabbit food never tasted so good.

1/4 cup grated carrots from the salad bar

2 tablespoons chunky peanut butter

1 tablespoon raisins

1 tablespoon orange juice

Stir together and serve on bread or with crackers.

Makes 8 servings.

THAI TAKEOUT (HOLD THE TAKEOUT)

Too busy with studying to make it to dinner? Thai-dy up your notes while you nosh on this delish meal-in-a-bowl.

1 cup rice

2 tablespoons peanut butter

1 teaspoon soy sauce

Cook the rice according to the directions on the package. Add the peanut butter and soy sauce, making sure that each grain of rice is coated. Clump together with your hands and eat!

Makes 1 serving.

PBR CRISPY TREATS

No, not the cheap beer. You *could* pair that with this tasty treat, but we recommend a tall, frosty glass of soy milk.

1 cup light corn syrup

1 cup sugar

1 cup smooth peanut butter

6 cups puffed rice cereal

Olive oil or vegan margarine, for greasing

Mix the corn syrup, sugar, and peanut butter in a container that can be microwaved. Heat slowly until the sugar dissolves, stirring every minute or so. Remove from microwave and stir the cereal in right away. Spread into a greased pan, and chill until firm. Cut and eat!

Makes 4 servings.

FINALS WEEK FUDGE

It's delicious, but it won't get you an A on your calculus exam.

3/4 cup vegan margarine

1 cup peanut butter

1 3/4 cups powdered sugar

Olive oil or vegan margarine, for greasing

Put the margarine in a bowl and nuke for 30 seconds, or until mostly melted. Stir in the peanut butter right away, while the bowl and margarine are still warm. Add the powdered sugar a little bit at a time, mixing well. Pour into a greased 9 × 9-inch pan and put in the fridge for at least 30 minutes. Cut into squares and serve.

Makes 4 servings.

PB BOMBS

Take one every hour to relieve symptoms of bombed tests. Warning: Will not get you through medical school.

1 cup vegan margarine

3 1/2 cups powdered sugar

2 cups graham cracker crumbs

3/4 cup peanut butter

Melt the margarine in the microwave—about 90 seconds—then mix everything together in a big bowl. Using your hands, roll the dough into golf ball–sized cookies. Chill in the fridge before serving.

Makes 4 servings.

FROZEN FRAT BALLS

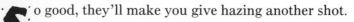

So good, they'll make you give hazing another shot.

1 (28-ounce) jar creamy peanut butter

3 cups powdered sugar

1 bag chocolate chips

Using your hands (c'mon, it's fun!), thoroughly smoosh the peanut butter and the powdered sugar together in a bowl, forming a dough. Roll 1-inch balls with the dough and place on a cookie sheet that's been covered with parchment or wax paper. Freeze for at least an hour. Remove from the freezer and set aside. Put the chocolate chips in a bowl and nuke for 1 minute. Stir. Heat for another 30 seconds, if necessary, and stir until smooth. Spoon onto the peanut-butter balls and freeze for at least an hour. Store in a cool, dry place.

Makes 4 servings.

ANTS ON A BLOG

A quick and healthy snack for all you die-hard bloggers too busy typing away to make a meal.

2 stalks celery, cut into sticks

1 small box raisins

4 tablespoons peanut butter

Spread the peanut butter on the celery and top with raisins.

Makes 1 serving.

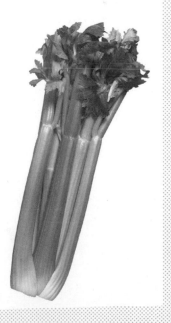

DIRTY HIPPIE TRAIL MIX

You may not be a granola kid, but after eating this amazing snack, you might just enjoy the scent of patchouli a little more.

- 1 cup pretzel sticks, broken in half
- 1 cup raisins
- 1 cup Nature Valley Crunchy Peanut Butter Granola Bars, crumbled into small pieces
- 1/2 cup sunflower kernels

Put everything in a gallon-size plastic bag and shake until completely mixed.

Makes 4 servings.

MYSTERY BARS

Are they breakfast? Are they dessert? Who cares?

7 cups of your fave crunchy vegan cereal

1 1/2 cups dried fruits

1 teaspoon cinnamon

3/4 cup brown rice syrup or agave nectar

3/4 cup peanut butter

2 tablespoons vegan margarine

Put the cereal, dried fruits, and cinnamon in a very large bowl and mix together. Put the syrup, peanut butter, and margarine in a large dish and nuke for 45 seconds to 1 minute, until almost melted. Stir till smooth and immediately pour over the cereal mixture, mixing everything together well. Pour into a 9 x 13-inch pan that's been sprayed with cooking spray. Freeze for at least 2 hours or overnight. Cut into squares and enjoy!

Makes 8 servings.

O BABY

O baby, I want more! And lucky for you, since they're home-made, you can eat as many as your little heart desires.

3 1/2 cups O-shaped vegan cereal

Handful vegan chocolate chips

1/2 cup maple syrup

1/2 cup peanut butter

Grease a pan and set aside. Put the cereal and chocolate chips in a large bowl and set aside. Put the maple syrup and peanut butter in a dish and nuke for about 30 seconds, until almost melted. Stir until smooth and immediately pour over the cereal mixture, stirring until all the cereal is coated. Press into the greased pan and refrigerate for at least 30 minutes. When cool, cut into squares.

Makes 4 servings.

PEANUT BUTTER CUP PIE

Chock-full of creamy chocolate and peanut butter, you'll love this vegan "Reese's" to pieces.

3/4 cup semisweet vegan chocolate chips, melted

2 (10.5-ounce) packages firm silken tofu

3/4 cup peanut butter

1 tablespoon maple syrup

9-inch graham cracker pie shell (most grocery stores have a vegan version)

1 ripe banana, thinly sliced

To melt the chocolate chips, place in a resealable freezer bag and put in the microwave for 1 minute or until the chips are melted. In a blender, puree the tofu, peanut butter, melted chocolate chips, and maple syrup until smooth. Cover the bottom of the pie crust with slices of banana. Pour the tofu mixture over the banana slices and chill for at least 2 hours.

Makes 8 servings.

WILD OATS CHOCOLATE COOKIES

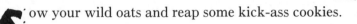**S**ow your wild oats and reap some kick-ass cookies.

- 1/2 cup vegan margarine
- 1/2 cup soy milk
- 4 tablespoon cocoa powder
- 2 cups sugar
- 1/2 cup peanut butter
- 3 cups quick oats

Nuke margarine, soy milk, cocoa powder, and sugar in large bowl on high for 3 minutes. Stir and then nuke for 2 more minutes. Remove from heat. Add peanut butter and stir until melted. Add oats and stir. Drop spoonfuls onto plates covered with wax paper. Refrigerate until cool.

Makes 8 servings.

PB&C NO-BAKE COOKIES

Cookies you don't have to slave over a stove for? Yes, please!

2/3 cup maple syrup

1/4 cup vegan shortening

1/4 cup cocoa powder

1/2 cup peanut butter

1 teaspoon cinnamon

2 cups rolled oats

Put the syrup, shortening, and cocoa powder in a bowl and nuke for about 30 seconds. Add peanut butter and nuke for an additional 45 seconds. Stir right away and continue stirring until combined. Add the cinnamon and oats and stir until well combined. Drop onto wax paper and put in the fridge for at least a half an hour before serving.

Makes 4 servings.

SALADS

Faux meats, sesame seeds, red beans, chickpeas, marinated tofu, nuts, orange segments—anything goes when it comes to these salads! We make things super-easy for you by letting you in on all the right fixins to make a ridiculously awesome-looking salad that will get all your friends begging you for a bite. A big bowl of one of these numbers can certainly rock your world!

DID YOU KNOW?

Vegetarianism is the ultimate weight-loss diet, since vegetarians are one-third as likely to be obese as meat-eaters are, and vegans are about one-tenth as likely to be obese. On average, vegans are 10 to 20 percent lighter than meat-eaters.

"OPEN A CAN" BEAN SALAD

If you have time to open five cans, well then, your lunch is basically made. You're welcome.

1 (15-ounce) can black beans

1 (15-ounce) can black-eyed peas

1 (15-ounce) can chickpeas

1 (15.5-ounce) can corn

1 tablespoon chopped chives

1 (14.5-ounce) can diced tomatoes (with peppers and onions is best)

1 (8-ounce) bottle Italian dressing

Put the beans and corn in a large colander and rinse well. Drain most of the liquid from the canned tomatoes. Combine all the ingredients in a large bowl and pour in about half the bottle of dressing (more if you want, to your own taste, but it shouldn't be soupy). Stir together and serve.

Makes 4 servings.

NOTE:

It's even tastier if you let it sit in the fridge and marinate for a couple of hours. This will make a week's worth of lunches.

LEAFY NUGGETS

A painless way to get your greens. Kind of like "studying" while watching TV.

1 (16-ounce) bag of pre-washed salad greens
1 (10-ounce) box vegan chicken patties
Vegan salad dressing, to taste

Dump the lettuce onto a plate and set aside. Nuke the chicken patties (as many or as few as you would like) until heated through, about a minute for each patty. Cut or tear up the patties and scatter over the lettuce. Toss with your favorite dressing. Enjoy!

Makes 2 servings.

LIP SMACKIN' THAI VEGGIES

The splash of lime will have you puckering up as much as your serial lip-locking suitemate—no lip balm required.

2 cups chopped/sliced mixed veggies from the salad bar
  (e.g., zucchini, bell peppers, onions)
Some bean sprouts from the salad bar
1/2 cup chopped nuts
1 tablespoon lime juice (fresh or from the squirt bottle)
1 tablespoon olive oil
1/2 teaspoon salt

Put everything in a huge bowl and toss together. Crunch away!

Makes 1 serving.

STRAWBERRY FIELD GREENS FOREVER

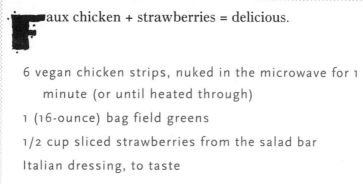

Faux chicken + strawberries = delicious.

6 vegan chicken strips, nuked in the microwave for 1
   minute (or until heated through)
1 (16-ounce) bag field greens
1/2 cup sliced strawberries from the salad bar
Italian dressing, to taste

Tear up the chicken and place in a bowl. Add the other ingredients and toss to coat.

Makes 2 servings.

RUSH WEEK GREEK SALAD

ll of the fun of going Greek with no bothersome hazing.

1 (16-ounce) package firm tofu, cut into 1-inch cubes

Italian dressing, to taste

8–10 cherry tomatoes

1 cup cucumber slices

1/2 cup black Greek olives, pitted

1 (16-ounce) bag lettuce (your choice)

Pour the dressing over the tofu in a large bowl and refrigerate for at least 1 hour. Add the tomatoes, cucumbers, and olives and toss to coat. Serve on the lettuce.

Makes 1 serving.

IN A PICKLE CHICKPEA SALAD

Remember that time you hooked up with your roommate's ex? This salad is like that—scandalous, yet it makes you feel oh-so-good!

- 1 (15-ounce) can chickpeas, drained and rinsed
- 1 cup celery, finely chopped (don't forget, salad bars come in handy for these things)
- 2 teaspoons onion powder
- 1–2 tablespoons nutritional yeast flakes
- Dill pickle relish, to taste
- Salt, to taste
- Vegan mayonnaise, to taste

Mix all the ingredients, except the mayo, together, mashing the chickpeas slightly as you mix. Once it's mixed to a soft, spreadable consistency, add the mayo until the salad is as moist as you like. Eat as is, or use on top of crackers or in a sandwich.

Makes 2 servings.

SKINNY CHICK CHICKPEA SALAD

Isn't it time you ditched the Freshman 15? Now go fill up on this easy, tasty salad!

1 (15-ounce) can chickpeas, drained

1 1/2 cups celery, diced (usually can find on any salad bar)

1/2 cup vegan mayonnaise

2 tablespoons lemon juice (fresh or from the squirter)

1 teaspoon garlic powder

1 teaspoon onion powder

Salt and pepper, to taste

Pita (optional)

Mix the chickpeas and celery. Add the remaining ingredients and season with salt and pepper. Serve in pita pockets or as an individual salad.

Makes 2 servings.

SPICY WATERMELON SALAD

You know what they say: You are what you eat. This salad will show people that you're not just sweet, you have a bit of an edge, too.

4 cups cubed watermelon

1 large cucumber, peeled and cubed

1/2 (4-ounce) can minced jalapeños

2 tablespoons white vinegar

2 tablespoons lime juice (fresh or from the squirt bottle)

Salt, to taste

Combine all the ingredients in a large bowl. Gently toss to coat. Chill for at least 1 hour and serve cold.

Makes 2 servings.

FRUIT SALAD ON THE FLY

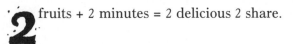

2 fruits + 2 minutes = 2 delicious 2 share.

1 orange, peeled

4 strawberries, washed

1 tablespoon lime juice (fresh or from squirt bottle)

Cut the orange and the strawberries into bite-sized pieces. Place in a bowl. Sprinkle with the lime juice and stir to combine. Enjoy!

Makes 1 serving.

CUKE–CHICK SALAD

Chickpeas and cucumbers make a much better duo than you and your last lab partner.

2 cucumbers, sliced

1/2 (15-ounce) can chickpeas

1 teaspoon onion powder

1/4 cup distilled vinegar

Salt and pepper, to taste

Put the cucumbers and chickpeas in a bowl. Add the onion powder and vinegar and stir everything together.

Makes 2 servings.

"GOES BOTH WAYS" CHICK SALAD

All we're saying is that this versatile salad is just as happy in a pita pocket as it is on a bed of lettuce leaves. Get your mind out of the gutter!

1 (8-ounce) package vegan chicken, shredded or diced

3 teaspoons dill-pickle relish

1 cup vegan mayonnaise

1 teaspoon black pepper

1 teaspoon garlic powder

Salt, to taste

Mix the chicken and dill-pickle relish together in a bowl. Add the mayo and mix. Add the seasonings and mix again. Serve on a salad, in a pita pocket, etc.

Makes 2 servings.

EXCLAMATION POINT EGGLESS SALAD

There are no periods in this salad. *Chicken* periods…also known as eggs. Yeah, we'd rather eat tofu, too.

1 (16-ounce) package extra-firm tofu, pressed and diced

1 1/4 cups vegan mayonnaise

1 cup nutritional yeast

1 teaspoon salt

1 teaspoon pepper

Mustard, to taste

Mix all the ingredients together in a bowl. Serve with pita wedges, on a sandwich, etc.

Makes 2 servings.

SLICE OF LIFE CHEF SALAD

Chef salads are usually big plates of dead things with a little lettuce. We guarantee that our version is death-free.

1 (16-ounce) bag salad greens

4 slices vegan ham

2 slices vegan turkey

10 cherry tomatoes

1/2 cup vegan cheddar cheese, shredded or cubed

1/4 cup vegan bacon bits

Vegan salad dressing, to taste

Place all the dry ingredients into a large bowl and toss together. Add dressing and toss again. Enjoy!

Makes 2 servings.

NUKE-LEAR MELTDOWN CHILI TACO SALAD

So named because you nuke it…and it melts. Shut up—this is damn delicious, and you know it.

1 (15-ounce) can chili beans in sauce

1 (12-ounce) bag veggie burger crumbles

4 slices vegan cheddar cheese

Tortilla chips

1 bag shredded lettuce

1/2 cup salsa

Jalapeños, to taste

Place the beans and the veggie burger crumbles in a large bowl. Nuke for 3 minutes. Top with the cheese and nuke for another 30 seconds, or until melted.

Place some tortilla chips on two plates. Top each plate of chips with half the chili mixture, then top with lettuce, salsa, and jalapeños.

Makes 2 servings.

CORNY SALAD

This salad is corny in the filled-with-corn-deliciousness kinda sense—not in the embarrassing-joke-Dad-tells-to-your-friends kinda sense.

    3 tablespoons olive oil

    2 teaspoons lime juice (fresh or from bottle)

    1 teaspoon sugar

    1/2 teaspoon salt

    1/4 teaspoon pepper

    2 cups frozen corn, thawed

    2 cups cherry tomatoes, halved

    1 cup peeled, chopped cucumber

Mix together the olive oil, lime juice, sugar, salt, and pepper in a large bowl. Add the corn, tomatoes, and cucumber and stir until fully combined.

Makes 2 servings.

ULTIMATE FRISBEE FRUIT SALAD

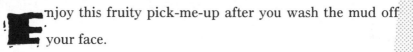njoy this fruity pick-me-up after you wash the mud off your face.

- 1 (16-ounce) plastic tub of pre-cut fruit of your choice
- 1/2 bunch of red seedless grapes
- 1 (20-ounce) can diced pineapple, drained
- 2 (6-ounce) containers vegan yogurt

Mix together and enjoy!

Makes 2 servings.

MIDTERM MACARONI SALAD

Just what you need to keep you focused and restore your sanity when your eyes start to blur and you can't stop mumbling about the 500 pages you have left to read before your midterm tomorrow.

1 (16-ounce) box macaroni

2 heaping teaspoons Dijon mustard

1 1/2 cups vegan mayonnaise

1/2 (10-ounce) bag shredded carrots

1/2 cup peas, nuked

1/4 cup chopped chives

Salt, to taste

Place the macaroni in a 64-ounce container and pour in water until macaroni is completely submerged (about 3/4 of the way full). Microwave on high for 5 minutes, stir, and repeat until macaroni is tender, generally about 10 to 12 minutes. While the macaroni is heating up, mix the mustard and mayonnaise together and add salt as needed. Drain all the water from the macaroni, and then add the carrots, peas, and chives to the macaroni. Top with the mayo/mustard sauce. Mix until well coated and refrigerate until ready to serve.

Makes 4 servings.

CHICK FLICK SALAD

Guys, invite your girlfriend over and eat this Italian salad while watching a romantic comedy, and we guarantee she'll be all over you like…er…salad dressing on a salad?

1 (8-ounce) bag vegan chicken or steak strips

1 bag lettuce

1 (10-ounce) bag shredded carrots

10 cherry tomatoes

1 tablespoon lemon juice (fresh or from a squirt bottle)

2 tablespoons olive oil

Salt and pepper, to taste

Nuke the meat for about 2 minutes, or until hot. Set aside. Mix all the veggies together in a large bowl and add the lemon juice, olive oil, salt, and pepper. Toss the salad until the veggies are well coated. Top with the meat and serve.

Makes 2 servings.

FAKIN' BACON 'N ORANGE SPINACH SALAD

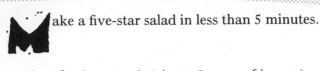ake a five-star salad in less than 5 minutes.

1 bag fresh spinach (about 6 cups of leaves)

1 orange, peeled and sliced into thin rounds

1 tablespoon sesame seeds

2 tablespoons seasoned rice vinegar

1 tablespoon orange juice concentrate

1 tablespoon water

1 tablespoon vegan bacon bits

Wash the spinach leaves and dry with paper towels. Place in a bowl along with the orange slices. Put the sesame seeds in a blender and grind into a powder. Add the vinegar, orange juice concentrate, and water into the blender and blend to mix. Pour over the salad and add the bacon bits. Toss before serving.

Makes 2 servings.

FIELD OF GREENS

Even easier than falling asleep in Statistics.

Field greens (about half a box or bag, or 1/2 pound)

1 (15-ounce) can chickpeas, drained and rinsed

1/2 cup sunflower seeds

1 cucumber, peeled and chopped (can use slices from the salad bar)

1/2 (10-ounce) bag of shredded carrots

Mix everything together and top with your favorite salad dressing.

Makes 2 servings.

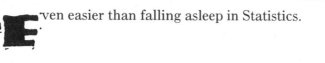

BLACK BEAN AND CORN SALAD (EXTENDED DANCE MIX)

If your taste buds wanna dance, here's the extended mix.

1/4 cup balsamic vinegar

2 tablespoons vegetable oil

1/2 teaspoon salt

1/2 teaspoon sugar

1/2 teaspoon pepper

1 (15-ounce) can black beans, drained and rinsed

1 (8.75-ounce) can corn, drained

1 (15-ounce) can diced tomatoes with chiles

1 teaspoon chives

Hot sauce, to taste

Mix all of the ingredients together and chill before serving.

Makes 2 servings.

NOTE:

This also makes an excellent dip served with tortilla chips.

BLACK BEAN AND CORN SALAD (SALSA REMIX)

O K, this mix is dedicated to all you salsa lovers out there.

1 (15-ounce) can black beans, drained and rinsed

1 (8.75-ounce) can corn, drained

6 tablespoons lime juice (fresh or from a squirt bottle)

5 tablespoons olive oil

1 tablespoon chives

1/2 cup salsa

Salt and pepper, to taste

Mix everything together. Cover and let chill in the fridge before serving.

Makes 2 servings.

SAFFI'S CHICK SALAD

Tabbouleh's grainy friend. Just as refreshing as tabbouleh without being bulgur.

1/2 (15-ounce) can chickpeas, drained and rinsed

1 1/2 cups cooked rice

1 tablespoon chives

1 long English cucumber, peeled and finely chopped (you can it get pre-sliced at the salad bar)

4 tablespoons dried parsley

1/3 cup lemon juice (fresh or from a squirt bottle)

1/3 cup olive oil

1 teaspoon salt

1/2 teaspoon pepper

Toss everything together in a large bowl and dig in!

Makes 2 servings.

DIRTY CHICK (PEA) CLEAN-UP SALAD

You had pizza and beer for every meal over the weekend. Clean up your act with this healthy and satisfying "cleanse" meal.

  1 (15.5-ounce) can chickpeas, drained and rinsed
  1/4 cup diced celery (go to your salad bar and grab some if you don't want to dice it yourself)
  1 Red Delicious or Gala apple, cored and diced
  Salt, to taste

Mix all the ingredients together and serve.

Makes 1 serving.

SLAW IN THE RAW

Your parents will be *much* happier being presented with this salad instead of that nude charcoal sketch you posed for in art class when you needed extra cash.

1 (16-ounce) bag shredded cabbage

1/2 cup roasted sunflower seeds or chopped nuts

1/2 cup vegan mayonnaise

1/2 cup lemon juice

Salt and pepper, to taste

Place all the ingredients in a large mixing bowl and stir to combine. Chill for 30 minutes, then serve.

Makes 2 servings.

STALKER FRUIT SALAD

Share this salad with your stalker—maybe if you're nice to him, he'll go away.

2 apples, cored and cut into quarters

1/2 cup water

1/2 cup soy milk

1 cup peanuts

2 cups cubed fresh fruit (try pears, cantaloupe, bananas — whatever you like) or canned fruit salad, drained

Handful of raisins

Blend the apples and 1/4 cup of water in a food processor (a blender will do in a pinch—just cut your apples into the smallest pieces possible). Add the soy milk, peanuts, and enough of the remaining water to reach a smooth consistency. Divide the fruit into four bowls and top with the peanut cream mixture. Sprinkle with raisins and serve.

Makes 4 servings.

KINESIOLOGY 101 SALAD

You *thought* you were done with P.E. in high school. Boy, were you wrong. At least this salad won't weigh you down while you're forced to do push-ups.

1 bag field greens salad

1/4 cup shredded carrots (you can buy them pre-shredded)

1/4 cup shredded cabbage (you can buy a bag of pre-shredded cabbage coleslaw)

1/4 cup sliced fresh mushrooms

1/4 cup chopped walnuts

Salad dressing, to taste

Combine all the ingredients in a bowl, toss together, and eat!

Makes 2 servings.

SOUPS AND STEWS

A hearty soup, chili, or stew can comfort you better than your roomie, your significant other, your toastiest microwaved socks, or even your mom. They leave you satisfied and warm—even if you're alone in your dorm room instead of sitting around the family table back home. Note: Invite a friend over, or the homeless dude on the bench on the quad, and you can do some old-fashioned bonding over asparagus soup. Everyone does that, right? It's not just us?

DID YOU KNOW?

A lifelong vegetarian saves around 760 chickens, 5 cows, 20 pigs, 29 sheep, 46 turkeys, 15 ducks, 7 rabbits, and half a ton of fish.

SPRINGTIME IN ASPARAGUS SOUP

Have you heard that green is the new black? Well, it's also the new soup.

- 2 teaspoons onion powder
- 2 tablespoons vegan margarine
- 1 (10-ounce) package frozen cut asparagus (you can also use fresh)
- 1 cup vegetable broth
- 1 dash garlic powder
- 1 dash pepper
- 1 cup plain soy milk

Mix all of the ingredients, except the soy milk, together in a bowl and nuke, covered, for 10 to 12 minutes. Remove from the microwave, let cool, and pour into a blender, pureeing until smooth. Return the mixture to a bowl, stir in the soy milk, and nuke until heated through.

Makes 2 servings.

"ME SO CORNY" THAI TOMATO SOUP

A "maize"ingly tasty and easy to make. Did we mention that this is supposed to be corny?

1 (10.7-ounce) can condensed tomato soup

1 (13-ounce) can condensed coconut milk

1 (15-ounce) can sweet corn (can substitute baby corn if preferred)

1 small bunch fresh cilantro, chopped (optional)

Salt and pepper, to taste

Mix all the ingredients in a container. Heat, partially covered, for 2 minutes. Stir. Repeat this process until the soup is thoroughly heated and well mixed.

Makes 4 servings.

CHEAPSKATE CHILI AND BEAN STEW

If you're strapped for cash, don't harvest your organs; buy kidney beans instead.

1 (15-ounce) can black beans (undrained)

1 (15-ounce) can kidney beans (undrained)

1 (15-ounce) can black-eyed peas (undrained)

1/2 cup chickpeas (undrained)

1 (14-ounce) can diced tomatoes (with juice)

1 (15-ounce) can enchilada sauce (preferably green-chili style)

Sea salt and fresh ground pepper, to taste

Corn or tortilla chips

Put all of the ingredients in a bowl (except for the corn or tortilla chips) and microwave on high for 4 minutes or until hot. Serve with chips.

Makes 4 servings.

HAAS PARTY AVOCADO SOUP

Tired of the same old played-out house party? Print up some flyers and tell the gang the soup's on at your place this Saturday night. Okay, don't actually make flyers, but double the batch if you're nice enough to share!

2 Haas avocados, cut in half and pits removed

2 cups soy milk

1 tablespoon lime juice (fresh or from a squirt bottle)

Salt and pepper, to taste

Scoop the avocado flesh into a bowl and mash it up. Mix in the soy milk and heat in the microwave for 2 minutes. Take the bowl out and add the lime juice, salt, and pepper, and heat for another 2 minutes. Eat.

Makes 2 servings.

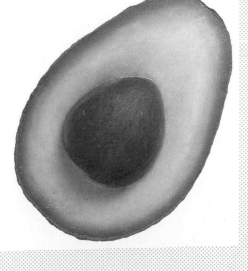

PJ PUMPKIN SOUP

Yup, you can pretend to be fancy while staying in your PJs. Don't act like you ever change out of your PJs anyway.

1 (15-ounce) can pumpkin puree

1 cup vegetable broth

1 tablespoon olive oil

1 cup plain soy milk

Salt and pepper, to taste

Combine all of the ingredients in a bowl and mix well. Nuke for 3 minutes, or until hot. Stir again and serve!

Makes 2 servings.

SASSY-ASS SOUTHWEST CHILI

A Mexi-Texi treat that'll sass your taste buds like a Texas beauty queen in her terrible 'tweens.

1/2 cup veggie burger crumbles

1 (15-ounce) can vegan chili or 2 cups pre-made vegan chili

1 (8-ounce) can mushrooms, stems and pieces, drained

1 (15-ounce) can diced tomatoes (look for one that's Mexican/chili style)

Grated vegan cheese, to taste

Taco seasoning, to taste

Mix all of the ingredients together and microwave until hot, 1 1/2 to 2 minutes.

Makes 4 servings.

PEACE RALLY PEA SOUP

C'mon, give peas a chance!

1 (12-ounce) package frozen peas

Water, to cover

1/2 to 1 cup vegetable broth

Pinch each of sugar, salt, and pepper

1/4 cup vegan sour cream

Cook the peas in the microwave until tender but not overly wrinkly, about 45 seconds to 1 minute. Drain, place in a blender, and whir until soup-like in texture, adding the veggie broth as necessary (you want a nice thick soup, so don't add too much). Remove from the blender and put back into the dish you micro-waved the peas in, adding the sugar, salt, and pepper. Heat through, about 1 minute. Divide into bowls, and swirl a little sour cream into each before serving!

Makes 2 servings.

FRENCH 101 LUNCH

So you're stuck in your dorm room studying for a French exam and listening to your roommate blast hip-hop. Pretend you're sitting in a French café on a cold, rainy day with this *délicieux* lunch. Beret and cynicism optional.

1 (19-ounce) can lentil soup

1 vegan sausage patty

1 baguette, split

Dijon mustard, to taste

Pour the soup into a bowl, nuke until hot, and remove from the microwave. Nuke the sausage patty until hot, about 45 seconds. Spread the mustard on the baguette and add the sausage. Dip into the soup. Bon appétit!

Makes 1 serving.

SPOTLIGHT ON: RAMEN

Ramen is likely one of those foods you've counted on more times than you can remember. When you're broke and hungry, ramen is there for you. Why not do something nice for ramen in return—dress it up! There's an endless number of things you can do to deck out your ramen, so try all of our suggestions, and then get creative and make up your own!

DID YOU KNOW?

Meat, dairy products, and eggs are completely devoid of fiber and complex carbohydrates, the nutrients that we're supposed to be consuming more of, and are laden with saturated fat and cholesterol, which make us fat and lethargic in the short term and lead to clogged arteries and heart attacks in the long term.

ANCIENT JAPANESE NOODLE SECRET SALAD

The secret? It's cheap, easy, and damn good.

1/4 cup vinegar

1/4 cup sugar

1 teaspoon soy sauce

1/4 cup vegetable oil

2 packages ramen noodles (seasoning packets not needed)

1/2 pound lettuce of your choice, shredded

1 (10-ounce) can mandarin orange segments, drained

1/4 cup slivered almonds

In a bowl, mix together the vinegar, sugar, soy sauce, and oil to make the dressing. Nuke until the sugar dissolves, about 1 minute. Mix well and let cool. Crush the ramen noodles in the packages, and then pour them into the salad dressing. Dump the lettuce on a plate or in a bowl, sprinkle the oranges and almonds on top, and top with the dressing/ramen mixture. Enjoy!

Makes 2 servings.

RAMEN HOLIDAY

Ramen for those fancier occasions.

1 package ramen (try Top Ramen Oriental flavor)
1 cup frozen mixed Italian veggies

Place the ramen noodles and veggies in a bowl. Add water according to the directions on the ramen package and nuke for 4 minutes, or until the veggies are hot. Add the seasoning packet and eat. Yum!

Makes 1 serving.

"PIMP MY RAMEN" NOODLES

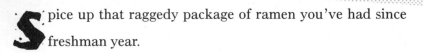

Spice up that raggedy package of ramen you've had since freshman year.

1 package ramen (try Top Ramen Oriental flavor)
1 heaping tablespoon peanut butter
1 tablespoon Sriracha hot chili sauce

Crush the ramen and place in a large bowl. Cover with water and stir in the seasoning packet. Nuke for 4 minutes, remove from the microwave, and add the peanut butter and chili sauce, mixing well.

Makes 1 serving.

NOTE:

Best when served topped with fresh bean sprouts and crushed peanuts.

RENT'S DUE "CHEEZY" RAMEN

You gotta pay the man, but you gotta eat, too. Stick it to him with this easy and filling bite you can easily afford after you search your roommate's pockets for change.

1 package ramen (try Top Ramen Oriental flavor)
2 tablespoons nutritional yeast

Cook the noodles according to the directions on the package and drain the excess water. Add the seasoning packet and nutritional yeast and stir.

Makes 1 serving.

DORM-ROOM RAMEN DELIGHT

Tricked-out pasta for budding but broke-ass foodies.

1 package ramen (try Top Ramen Oriental flavor, minus the
    seasoning packet)
Water
1 teaspoon vegan margarine
Garlic powder, to taste
Salt and pepper, to taste
Nutritional yeast, to taste

Cook the ramen noodles in the microwave in just enough water
to cover them. Drain. Add the margarine and a sprinkle with the
garlic powder, salt, pepper, and nutritional yeast. Stir together
and eat.

Makes 1 serving.

FRESHASAURUS MEX RAMEN CASSEROLE

Everyone knows that ramen's been around since dinosaurs ruled the earth, so try this fresh take on a Cretaceous Period classic.

6 cups water

3 packages ramen noodles

2 (15-ounce) cans vegan chili

1 (15-ounce) can tomatoes

4–8 ounces shredded vegan cheese

Put water in a 3-quart casserole dish. Cover with a lid and nuke for 3 minutes. Remove from the microwave. Crush the ramen inside the packages, (you won't be needing the seasoning packets), and dump the noodles into the dish. Cover and nuke for 5 minutes, stirring halfway through. Remove and drain. Put the noodles back in the casserole dish, add the chili and the undrained tomatoes, and toss well. Cover and return to the microwave, nuking for 5 minutes or until hot throughout. Remove from the microwave, sprinkle with the cheese, replace the cover, and let stand until the cheese melts.

Makes 4 servings.

SAUCES AND DRESSINGS

The French have some pretty great ideas—you know, like the bicycle, the sewing machine, and more importantly, the French kiss—so you should listen to 'em when they say sauces and dressings can absolutely make or break a dish. Think about it: If you have the most amazing melt-in-your-mouth mashed potatoes and then pile some nasty-tasting gravy on top, your 'taters are ruined, right? We promise that our sauces and dressings will keep your dishes oh-so-lovely, or you can come to our office and we'll grovel at your feet and beg for your forgiveness. Okay, so maybe not. But we will pat you on the back and say, "Better luck next time, Champ."

DID YOU KNOW?

Meat-eaters consume more than twice the recommended amount of protein. In a series of comparative endurance tests conducted by Dr. Irving Fisher of Yale University, vegetarians performed twice as well as meat-eaters. When Dr. Fisher knocked down the non-vegetarians' protein consumption by 20 percent, their efficiency went up by 33 percent.

SUPER CHEEZY SAUCE

Carbalicious over rice or pasta, this sauce is cheesier than your roommate's corkboard collage of her high school friends.

1/3 cup nutritional yeast
1 tablespoon soy sauce
1 tablespoon olive oil
Enough water to make a sauce
Pepper, to taste

Blend all the ingredients together until smooth. Pop in the microwave for 1 minute, or until warm. Add liberally to cooked rice or pasta.

Makes 2 servings.

RAUNCHY DRESSING

Your roomie's sock is on the doorknob again, so you might as well order a pizza and make some ranch dressing to dip it in—it might be a while.

- 1 cup vegan mayonnaise (we recommend using 1/2 cup of Nayonaise and 1/2 cup of Veganaise)
- 1/4 cup soy milk
- 2 overflowing teaspoons dried parsley
- 1 1/2 teaspoons apple-cider vinegar
- 1/2 teaspoon salt
- 1/2 teaspoon garlic powder
- 1/2 teaspoon onion powder
- 1/2 teaspoon black pepper
- 1/4 teaspoon dill weed

Put all the ingredients in a blender and blend until creamy.

Makes 2 servings.

BAD-ASS BALSAMIC VINAIGRETTE

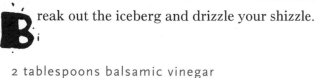reak out the iceberg and drizzle your shizzle.

- 2 tablespoons balsamic vinegar
- 2 tablespoons seasoned rice vinegar
- 2 tablespoons water
- 2 teaspoons garlic powder
- Olive oil, to taste

Mix all the ingredients together in a small bowl. Use on salads or to dip bread in.

Makes 2 servings.

"DRESS TO IMPRESS" CITRUS DRESSING

Drizzling this light and flavorful dressing over an ordinary salad is kinda the opposite of wearing your PJs to class. It's good to get dressed up now and then.

3/4 cup orange juice

6 tablespoons mustard

1 cup olive oil

Salt and pepper, to taste

Put all of the ingredients in a blender and blend until smooth. Serve over mixed greens or the salad of your choice.

Makes 8 servings.

THOUSAND-TIMES-BETTER SALAD DRESSING

ecause when else are you allowed to put mayo and ketchup on a salad?!

1 cup vegan mayonnaise

1/3 cup ketchup

3 tablespoons sweet pickle relish

1/2 teaspoon onion powder

1/4 teaspoon salt

1/8 teaspoon garlic powder

1 (4.25-ounce) can chopped green olives or chopped olives
  from the salad bar (optional)

Stir all the ingredients together in a bowl.

Makes 8 servings.

KETCHUP'S ROCKIN' TWIN

Who wants to cover or smother anything with those gross fructose-based fast-food packets glommed to the inside of your fridge door? It's all about going homemade.

1/3 cup ketchup

1/4 cup vegan mayonnaise

1/2 teaspoon mustard

1 dash salt

1 dash pepper

1 dash garlic powder

Stir together all the ingredients in a bowl. Refrigerate until serving.

Makes 2 servings.

NO-YOLK MAYO

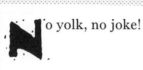o yolk, no joke!

1/2 cup soy milk

3 tablespoons lemon juice

1/4 teaspoon salt

1/4 teaspoon paprika

1/4 teaspoon yellow mustard

6 tablespoons vegetable oil

Put all the ingredients, except the oil, in a blender and blend on the lowest speed. With the blender running, gradually add the oil until the mixture starts to thicken. Continue blending until thickened and smooth. Transfer to a jar and store in the refrigerator.

Makes 8 servings.

DINNER

WARNING: Once you start making these dinner delights, the delicious aroma will waft down the hall and you'll need to fight the moochers off with a stick...or at least charge admission at the door. These dishes will fill you up and fool all of your friends into thinking you're a culinary genius.

DID YOU KNOW?

Many of history's greatest minds were vegetarian, such as: Pythagoras, Socrates, Plato, Clement of Alexandria, Plutarch, King Asoka, Leonardo da Vinci, Montaigne, Akbar, John Milton, Sir Isaac Newton, Emanuel Swedenbourg, Voltaire, Benjamin Franklin, Jean-Jacques Rousseau, Lamartine, Percy Bysshe Shelley, Ralph Waldo Emerson, Henry David Thoreau, Leo Tolstoy, George Bernard Shaw, Rabindranath Tagore, Mahatma Gandhi, Albert Schweitzer, and Albert Einstein.

SILENCE OF THE LAMBS SHEPHERD'S PIE

Why are the lambs quiet? 'Cuz they're not being turned into meat pies! "Beefy" enough to fool even the most cultured cannibals, so get the Chianti out and invite all of your Little Bo Peeps over for dinner.

- 2 servings of instant potatoes (read the ingredients to make sure they're vegan)
- 1 (12-ounce) package veggie burger crumbles
- 1 (14.5-ounce) can mixed veggies (peas and carrots), drained
- 1 (8.75-ounce) can of corn, drained
- 3 tablespoons vegetarian vegetable broth
- Salt and pepper, to taste

Cook the instant mashed potatoes according to the directions on the box. Set aside. Microwave the veggie burger crumbles for 1 1/2 minutes. Mix the veggies, crumbles, and veggie broth in a bowl. Top with mashed potatoes, sprinkle on salt and pepper, and nuke for another minute, or until hot.

Makes 4 servings.

WTF? WINGS

maze your meat-head friends with this "tastes-like-the-real-thing" alternative. So scrumptious, you'll have them dragging their knuckles to the nearest market to get their own faux fixins.

2 (8-ounce) bags vegan chicken strips

1/3 cup soy sauce

1 cup fine cracker crumbs

1/2 teaspoon garlic powder

1/8 teaspoon pepper

Thaw the chicken strips. Pour the soy sauce into a bowl and set aside. In another bowl, combine the cracker crumbs, garlic powder, and pepper. Dip the chicken in the soy sauce and then roll in the seasoned crumbs, coating evenly. Arrange on a plate and cover with paper towels. Microwave on high for 5 minutes or until hot. Serve with your favorite dipping sauce from the last chapter.

Makes 2 servings.

HALF-ASSED CHILI

When yummy chili is the goal but you don't want to spend more than 5 minutes making it happen, bust out this recipe. It's kind of like riding out those final three credits with a pottery class.

1 (16-ounce) jar salsa
1 (15-ounce) can chili beans, undrained
1 (15-ounce) can black beans, drained and rinsed
1 (8.75-ounce) can corn kernels, drained
1/2 (4-ounce) can jalapeños

Combine everything in a bowl. Cover and nuke until hot, about 4 minutes, stirring occasionally.

Makes 4 servings.

F-U TACOS

These tacos put the "fu" in tofu.

1 (12-ounce) package silken firm tofu

1 package vegan taco seasoning mix

1 (16-ounce) can vegetarian refried beans

1 package taco shells

Shredded lettuce, vegan cheese, tomato, etc. (optional)

Put the tofu and seasoning mix in a blender and blend until smooth. Transfer to a medium-sized bowl. Fold in the beans. Nuke for 2 to 3 minutes, or until hot, stirring halfway through. Fill the taco shells with the tofu mixture and top with your favorite taco toppers.

Makes 4 servings.

NO-BEEF STROGANOFF

So easy you can make this blindfolded, but don't hold it against us if you spill tomato sauce all over your room-mate's term paper.

1 (12-ounce) package
    veggie burger
    crumbles
1 cup sliced fresh
    mushrooms
1/4 cup tomato sauce
2 teaspoons onion
    powder

1 teaspoon mustard
1/2 teaspoon sugar
1/4 teaspoon salt
Pepper, to taste
1 cup vegan sour cream
1/4 to 1/2 cup soy milk
Rice or noodles,
    previously cooked

Empty the crumbles into a large microwave-safe bowl and nuke for about 2 minutes, stirring halfway through. They won't be heated all the way, but that's fine. Add everything else, except the sour cream, soy milk, and rice or noodles, to the bowl and nuke for 3 minutes, or until hot, stirring halfway through. Mix in the sour cream and soy milk right before serving. Serve over rice or noodles.

Makes 4 servings.

NO-GRIEF "BEEF" NOODLES

We promise, neither you nor any cow will be harmed in the making of these e-z, "cheesy," nuked noodles.

6 ounces noodles, uncooked

4 slices vegan cheese

1 (12-ounce) package veggie burger crumbles, thawed

Salt and pepper, to taste

2 tablespoons vegan mayonnaise

1 tablespoon water

Submerge the noodles in water in a bowl and nuke for 5 minutes. Stir and repeat until thoroughly cooked. Drain completely. Put the cheese, veggie burger crumbles, salt, pepper, mayonnaise, and water in a large bowl and stir together. Nuke for 1 minute. Stir, add the noodles, and nuke for 1 more minute, or until hot.

Makes 4 servings.

LEGUME VA-VA-VOOM

The ultimate impress-a-date-dish, we guarantee that dinner will go over really well. However, we can in no way promise that you won't be dealt the "friend card" during dessert.

6 cups brown rice, cooked

1–2 large, ripe avocados

1/2 (15-ounce) can lentils

1/2 cup chopped peanuts

Salt and pepper, to taste

4 large romaine lettuce leaves

After cooking the rice and before it cools completely, halve the avocados, remove the pits, scoop out the pulp, and mash it into the rice. When the ingredients have blended, add the lentils and peanuts. Season with salt and pepper. Serve portions on top of the washed romaine leaves. Bon appétit!

Makes 6 servings.

MICRO-RITOS

All you need is a microwave for an instant fiesta. Okay, some amigos and a bottle of tequila would be nice, too, but don't blame us if you get busted by the RA.

- 1 (8-ounce) bag vegan chicken or steak strips
- 1 (16-ounce) jar salsa
- 1 (15-ounce) can black or pinto beans
- 1 (10-ounce) package Mexican-style vegan cheese, grated
- 1 package (10-inch) tortillas
- 1 bag boil-in-bag brown or white rice (optional)

If you're including rice in the dish, make it first, then set aside to be combined with all the ingredients before serving. Nuke the "meat" for about 2 minutes, or until cooked through. Combine the beans, salsa (reserving a small bit to top off the burritos), meat, and cheese in bowl and nuke for about 2 minutes, or until hot. Nuke the tortillas between two damp paper towels for a few seconds to warm and soften. Spoon the mixture into the tortillas, top with some salsa, roll up, and eat.

Makes 4 servings.

"TASTES LIKE CHICKEN" STRIPS

Meaty enough to fool hardcore carnivores, but we promise—they're as fake as your I.D.

3/4 cup vegan mayonnaise

1/2 cup Italian salad dressing

2 tablespoons vinegar

2 tablespoons water

2 (8-ounce) bags vegan chicken strips

Mix everything but the chicken in a bowl. Pour the mixture into a large ziplock bag, add the chicken, and let marinate for 30 minutes. Place on a plate and nuke for 2 minutes. Optional: These are great on their own or served with rice.

Makes 4 servings.

NOT YOUR AVERAGE BURRITO

Stuffed with fake chicken, brown rice, and broccoli, this burrito is weirder than that kid in the single room down the hall with garlic cloves hanging from the ceiling. But it's delicious, trust us!

5 vegan chicken strips

1/4 cup brown rice, cooked (use microwaveable)

1/3 cup broccoli florets, frozen

1 (10-inch) tortilla

1/3 cup shredded vegan cheese

Salsa, to taste

Cook the chicken, brown rice, and broccoli in the microwave according to each package's instructions. Set aside. Warm the tortillas in the microwave for 10 seconds. Top each tortilla with the rice, broccoli, chicken, cheese, and salsa , roll into a burrito, and enjoy!

Makes 1 serving.

GREEN BEAN NO-HASSLE-ROLE

Quick and easy comfort food from the discomfort of your cramped kitchen.

1/2 cup vegan margarine

1/2 cup flour

1 1/2 cups vegan mushroom soup

1 tablespoon soy sauce

1/2 teaspoon garlic powder

2 tablespoons vegetable oil

1/4 cup nutritional yeast flakes

2 (14.5-ounce) cans French-style green beans, drained

1 (2.8-ounce) can French-fried onions

Put the margarine in a bowl and nuke for about 20 seconds, until almost completely melted. Stir until completely melted (you might need to nuke it for another 10 seconds or so). Add the flour and stir. Add the soup, soy sauce, and garlic powder, and stir until thoroughly mixed. Nuke for 2 minutes. Add the oil and nutritional yeast and stir until smooth. Pour the sauce into a small casserole dish, add the green beans and half the can of French onions, and stir to coat. Nuke for 5 minutes. Top with the remaining onions and then nuke for 5 minutes.

Makes 4 servings.

LEAVE-OUT-THE-NOODLES LASAGNA

No noodles? No problem! Stuff your stomach with this super-easy lasagna and get your Italian fix.

1 tablespoon lemon juice

2 teaspoons dried basil

3/4 teaspoon salt

1/2 teaspoon garlic powder

1 (16-ounce) package firm tofu, drained and mashed

1 (12-ounce) package vegan sausage, crumbled

1 or 2 (16-ounce) cans of artichoke hearts packed in water

1 (28-ounce) jar pasta sauce

1 (10-ounce) bag frozen peas, thawed

2 tablespoons olive oil

Mix the lemon juice, basil, salt, garlic powder and tofu together in a large bowl. Set aside. Nuke sausage in the microwave for 2 minutes or until warm. Drain the artichoke hearts, cut into pieces and set aside. Cover the bottom of a large bowl with pasta sauce. Toss in all of the ingredients and top with the remaining pasta sauce. Nuke for 5 minutes, or until hot.

Makes 4 servings.

LOTSA MOZZA PIZZA BAGELS

Hobbit-sized pizzas guaranteed to vanquish your munchies 'to Middle Earth.

1 (10-ounce) can tomato sauce or pizza sauce

1 bagel, sliced in half and toasted

Hot sauce, to taste

Garlic powder, to taste

Shredded vegan mozzarella "cheese"

Veggies (optional)

Spread tomato sauce on both halves of the bagel. Add a few drops of hot sauce and then sprinkle with garlic powder. Add the cheese and veggies (if desired) and nuke for about 30 seconds, or until the cheese is melted.

Makes 1 serving.

CHICK MAGNET "CHICKEN" CASSEROLE

Chicks totally dig a guy who cooks for them. This easy-to-make and downright impressive-looking dish is a sure thing, so how about laying off the cheap cologne there, Ace?

1 (16-ounce) package silken tofu, mashed

1/4 cup nutritional yeast

1 cup celery, diced

1 teaspoon garlic powder

1 teaspoon salt

1 teaspoon pepper

1 (15-ounce) can diced tomatoes with green chile peppers

1 bag tortilla chips

2 (8-ounce) bags vegan chicken strips

1 (10-ounce) block of cheddar-style vegan cheese

Combine the tofu, nutritional yeast, celery, garlic powder, salt, and pepper in a medium-sized bowl, stirring until the mixture is well blended. Add the tomatoes and stir. Set aside. In a lightly greased 2-quart casserole dish, layer one-third of the chips, one-half of the chicken, one-half of the tomato/tofu mixture, and one-third of the cheese. Repeat the layers, then top with the remaining tortilla chips and cheese. Cover the dish with waxed paper or a lid and nuke for 7 minutes. Uncover and nuke for 4 more minutes, or until heated thoroughly.

Makes 6 servings.

THE BURNING BIBIMBAP BOWL

A Korean-inspired meal in a bowl, guaranteed to bring on the burn. A good burn, though—not the kind that sends you to the campus clinic.

- 2 teaspoons hot pepper paste
- 2 teaspoons sesame tahini
- 2 teaspoons vegetable oil
- 2 teaspoons soy sauce
- 2 bowls microwaveable rice, cooked

Combine all of the ingredients, except the rice, in a small bowl. Split the cooked rice between two bowls, then add half of the mixture to each bowl of rice and mix well. Enjoy!

Makes 2 servings.

PANTRY RAID PASTA

Nothing to eat? Don't get your granny panties in a bunch. There are *always* noodles hiding in your cupboard. If not, run down the hall, burst into your neighbors' rooms, and raid their pantries.

1 (16-ounce) box elbow pasta
1 (15-ounce) can diced tomatoes
2 (8-ounce) bags vegan chicken strips
Salt and pepper, to taste

Put the pasta in a large bowl and fill the bowl with water until the pasta is submerged (you may need to split the pasta in half and do one half at a time). Cook on high for 5 minutes, stir, and repeat until tender. Drain the excess water. Set the drained pasta aside. Cut open the bag of chicken strips and place in the microwave. Cook for 2 minutes, or until heated through. Pour the pasta on a plate and top with the diced tomatoes, chicken, salt, and pepper. Heat for 1 more minute and voila!

Makes 4 servings.

AFTER DELIVERY HOURS STIR-FRY

Delivery hours are over and you're hungry. Make your own stir fry (no wok required)!

1 (16-ounce) bag mixed vegetables, frozen

1 (14-ounce) can baby corn

1 (8-ounce) can water chestnuts

1 (8-ounce) can bamboo shoots

Soy sauce, to taste

2 servings microwaveable rice, cooked

Dump the bag of veggies in bowl and nuke for 4 minutes or until warm. Add the corn, water chestnuts, and bamboo shoots and nuke for an additional 2 minutes. Add soy sauce and place veggies on top of rice.

Makes 4 servings.

ROAD TRIP RED BEANS AND RICE

Fill up with a hot and spicy punch of protein before you hit the road.

1 (16-ounce) can dark red kidney beans, drained

1 (14.5-ounce) can tomatoes, diced and drained

2 servings instant rice, cooked

1 (4-ounce) can green chiles

Hot sauce, to taste

Combine all of the ingredients together in a large bowl and heat in the microwave for 3 minutes, or until hot.

Makes 4 servings.

BETTER THAN THE "BELL" BURRITO

Yeah, you could just go to the drive-thru burrito joint, but why bother when you can make it at home?

2 (8-ounce) tubs vegan cream cheese

3/4 cup salsa

2 tablespoons hot sauce

Salt, to taste

1 tablespoon lime juice (fresh or from the squirt bottle)

1 avocado, mashed

6 (8-inch) flour tortillas

1 (16-ounce) bag fresh baby spinach

1 (14.5-ounce) can corn

1 (4-ounce) can sliced black olives

Combine the cream cheese, salsa, hot sauce, and salt in a medium sized bowl. In a small bowl, pour lime juice over sliced avocado to prevent browning. Spread 3 tablespoons of the cream cheese mix on each tortilla, place 2 rows of spinach leaves in the center of each tortilla, then top each row with avocado, corn, and black olives. Roll the tortillas up tightly. Top with salsa.

Makes 3 servings.

BROCKIN' RICE PILAF

Tastes like something from a fancy restaurant, without any of the fuss. Feel free to wipe your mouth on your sleeve.

1 cup microwaveable rice

1 1/2 (16-ounce) cans vegetarian vegetable broth

1 (10-ounce) bag frozen chopped broccoli

Salt and pepper, to taste

Cook the microwaveable rice in the vegetable broth instead of water (follow all other directions on the package). Take out and set aside. Cook the broccoli in the microwave for 4 minutes, or until heated. Mix the broccoli and rice together and add salt and pepper as needed.

Makes 4 servings.

GUAC WRAPS

A Mexican take on a lettuce wrap. Wash it down with a glass of orchata (cinnamon rice milk), close your eyes, and pretend you're in Mexico.

- 1/2 cup corn kernels
- 1/4 cup guacamole (buy from a store or use the recipe on page 218)
- 1/4 cup salsa
- 1 tablespoon lime juice (from squirt bottle or fresh)
- 1/2 teaspoon garlic powder
- 1/2 teaspoon onion powder
- 2 large lettuce leaves

Mix everything but the lettuce leaves together in a bowl. Divide in half and plop in the middle of the two lettuce leaves. Roll them up into burritos and eat.

Makes 1 serving.

PEAS 'N' RICE IS NICE

When you're short on time and dinner ideas, peas and rice is always nice. It's quick, cheap, and filling, so try not to doze off when you're done—you were in a hurry, remember?

1/2 (14.5-ounce) can peas
2 tablespoons canned diced tomatoes, juice drained
2 servings microwaveable rice, cooked
Garlic powder, to taste
Salt, to taste

Cook the rice according to package directions and set aside. Put the peas and tomatoes in a bowl and nuke for about 1 1/2 minutes, or until hot. Add the peas and tomatoes to the cooked rice and sprinkle on some garlic powder and salt. Mix together and eat.

Makes 2 servings.

RICHIE RICE

You can eat like royalty and still manage to pay off your student loans.

2 cups cooked rice

1 (14.5-ounce) can vegan butternut squash soup

1/2 cup vegan soy parmesan cheese

Garlic powder, to taste

Onion powder, to taste

Salt, to taste

Put everything in a large bowl, stir well, and nuke for about 1 1/2 minutes, or until hot. Stir before serving.

Makes 2 servings.

TACO CON CHILI

This seemingly random pairing of two foods is a match made in heaven. Unlike you and your freshman year roommate, who snored and didn't believe in showers.

3/4 cup homemade vegan chili

2 vegan taco shells

1/3 cup shredded lettuce

1/4 cup salsa

2 tablespoons vegan sour cream

Nuke the chili in a microwave-safe dish until heated through. Divide in half and place in the taco shells. Top with lettuce, salsa, and sour cream.

Makes 2 servings.

TEXAS RANGER ROLL-UPS

Chuck Norris doesn't eat these Tex-Mex roll-ups. He forces them into submission.

1 (15.5-ounce) can corn, drained

1 (15-ounce) can black beans, rinsed and drained

2 tablespoons lime juice (fresh or from a squirt bottle)

2 tablespoons orange juice

2 teaspoons chopped chives

2 teaspoons garlic powder

1/8 teaspoon salt

4 flour or corn tortillas

Salsa

Mix all the ingredients together, except the tortillas and the salsa. Spoon the mixture onto the tortillas, roll them up tightly, and top with salsa.

Makes 4 servings.

ALL-NIGHTER NACHOS

Bad news: Your ten-pager is due at 8 a.m. tomorrow and you haven't started it yet. Good news: Noshing on these zesty, protein-packed nachos will nix your chances of nodding off before you finish the footnotes.

1 (12-ounce) package veggie burger crumbles
Dash of oil
2 teaspoons onion powder
1 package taco seasoning
1 (16-ounce) jar chunky salsa
1 bag of your favorite tortilla chips

Nuke the crumbles in a large bowl until warm, about 1 minute. Stir in the remaining ingredients and serve with tortilla chips.

Makes 4 servings.

GIZMO'S GLAZED CHICK'N

Hungry like a gremlin after midnight? Squash those mad 'mogwai munchies with this sweet and tangy rice dish.

1/4 cup Italian dressing

2 tablespoons apricot preserves

2 (8-ounce) bags vegan chicken strips, thawed

Mix together the dressing and the preserves in a bowl. Put in a large resealable bag with the chicken and shake. Let sit in fridge for 30 minutes. Put on a plate and nuke for 30 seconds. Great alone or served with rice.

Makes 4 servings.

BY THE TEXTBOOK
TEMPEH TACOS

A textbook example of why tempeh should be used often and in large, delicious quantities.

3 (8-ounce) packages tempeh
1 package taco seasoning
1/4 cup water
Salsa
4 (10-inch) tortillas
Fixings of choice

Crumble the tempeh in a bowl and nuke for 2 minutes, or until hot. Add the water and taco seasoning. Stir it up and add as much salsa as you'd like. Scoop into the tortillas and add other fixings according to your taste, like lettuce, tomatoes, etc., and have a Tex-Mex kind of night.

Makes 4 servings.

CURE-ALL NOODLES

Move over, chicken soup. These creamy, comforting noodles have been proven to heal a variety of ailments, including but not limited to: failed tests, homesickness, hangovers, and cafeteria food-induced starvation.

1 (16-ounce) package pasta of your choice

1/2 (8-ounce) container vegan cream cheese

1/2 (12-ounce) container vegan sour cream

1/2 (28-ounce) jar pasta sauce

Cook the noodles by submerging them in water in a microwave-safe dish and nuking for about 5 minutes; stir and repeat until completely cooked. Drain and set aside. Mix together the remaining ingredients in a separate bowl and nuke for 1 minute. Place the noodles on a plate and top with the sauce.

Makes 4 servings.

MAKE A REAL MEAL "MEATY" SPAGHETTI

Can you survive on Twizzlers, Fruit Loops, and Red Bull? Uh, yeah. *Should* you? Hell, no!

1 (16-ounce) package spaghetti

1 (14-ounce) tube vegan sausage

1 tablespoon garlic powder

2 tablespoons olive oil

Italian herbs, to taste

Salt and pepper, to taste

1 (28-ounce) jar spaghetti sauce

Break the spaghetti in half, place in a bowl, and submerge in water. Nuke for 5 minutes, stir, and repeat until thoroughly cooked. Remove from the microwave, drain, and set aside. Break the sausage into bite-size pieces. Place in another bowl along with the garlic powder, olive oil, Italian herbs, salt, and pepper. Nuke for approximately 5 minutes, or until the sausage is sizzling. Pour in the jar of sauce. Cover loosely with plastic wrap and nuke for 1 to 2 minutes, or until hot, stirring halfway through. Toss the spaghetti with the sauce and serve.

Makes 4 servings.

AFTERPARTY AGLIO OLIO

Impress that hottie you brought back to your room after a long night out by making (and correctly pronouncing) this steamy Italian snack. Need a hint, Romeo? It's ah-leo oh-leo.

1/2 (16-ounce) box spaghetti
1 tablespoon olive oil
1 (14.5-ounce) can diced tomatoes, drained
1/2 teaspoon salt
1 teaspoon garlic powder
1 tablespoon vegan margarine

Submerge the noodles in water and cook in the microwave for 5 minutes, stir, and repeat until tender. Meanwhile, mix the oil, tomatoes, salt, and garlic powder. Take the spaghetti out of the microwave, drain, and toss onto a plate. Add the margarine to the oil mixture and microwave until the margarine is melted. Pour over the spaghetti and toss.

Makes 2 servings.

BBCUTIE CHICKPEAS

 aucier than a pissed-off Southern sorority girl, y'all.

2 (15-ounce) cans chickpeas, drained

1/2 bottle BBQ sauce

1/2 teaspoon onion powder

Mix chickpeas, BBQ sauce, and onion powder together in a big bowl. Nuke on high for 2 minutes. Stir. Serve over rice or noodles.

Makes 4 servings.

NIGHT OWL NACHOS

Whether you're cramming for a test or up 'til dawn downloading music, these "cheesy" nachos are the perfect culinary companion for any all-nighter.

1 (15-ounce) can black beans, drained

1 cup salsa

1/4 cup nutritional yeast

1 bag tortilla chips

1 (10-ounce) can diced tomatoes

1 teaspoon chopped chives

1/4 cup lettuce

3 tablespoons vegan sour cream

Salt and pepper, to taste

Place the black beans in a bowl and heat in the microwave for 2 minutes. In another, smaller container, mix the salsa and the nutritional yeast together and heat for 1 minute. Arrange the chips on a plate and top with the beans, salsa-yeast mixture, diced tomatoes, chives, lettuce, and sour cream.

Makes 3 servings.

CUTTING CLASS QUESADILLA

Be honest with yourself. If you're not going to go to class, at least learn *something*…like how to make a decent meal.

2 (10-inch) tortillas

2–3 slices vegan cheese (Tofutti works best in this case)

Salsa and vegan sour cream, optional

Place one tortilla on a plate. Place the slices of cheese on the tortilla and then top with the other tortilla. Microwave for 1 minute or until cheese is melted. Cut into thirds and top with salsa and "sour cream" (optional). Enjoy!

Makes 2 servings.

EXAM WEEK FUEL

Yes, it *is* perfectly possible to survive on pizza quesadillas for an entire week. Just be sure to supplement with plenty of soda, coffee, and spontaneous sleep deprivation-induced dorm room dance parties for a balanced diet.

2 (6-inch) flour tortillas
1/4 cup shredded cheddar-style vegan cheese
1/4 cup shredded mozzarella-style vegan cheese
2 slices vegan turkey lunch meat
1 tablespoon pizza or tomato sauce

Place one of the tortillas on a plate. Spoon 2 tablespoons each of the cheddar- and mozzarella-style cheeses over the tortilla. Cover with the turkey slices. Spread the sauce over the turkey and top with the remaining cheeses. Place the second tortilla on top. Cook in microwave until the cheese melts, about 1 1/2 minutes. Allow to cool before cutting into wedges.

Makes 1 serving.

BETTER THAN TAKEOUT TOFU

When you've spent your last dollar on this semester's books, try this tasty dish. You'll never need delivery again!

1 (16-ounce) package firm or extra-firm tofu

1 tablespoon lemon juice

Soy sauce, to taste

1 teaspoon garlic powder

Chop the tofu into cubes or strips and microwave for 2 minutes, or until hot. Add lemon, soy sauce, and garlic to the tofu and mix until well-coated. Serve over microwave rice or eat as is.

Makes 4 servings.

DROPOUT SPAGHETTI

You don't even have to boil water for this, which automatically makes it easier than your chem lab.

4 ounces pasta

3/4 cup favorite vegan spaghetti sauce

3/4 cup veggie burger crumbles, thawed completely

Submerge the pasta in water in a large bowl and nuke for 5 minutes. Stir and repeat until thoroughly cooked. Remove from the microwave and drain. Put back in the bowl, add the sauce and the crumbles, and nuke for 1 minute.

Makes 1 serving.

"CHEAT MEAT" LOVERS BBQ PIZZA

It's okay to cheat. Really. Loaded with tons of faux meat and smothered in mouthwatering BBQ sauce, cheating never tasted so good!

- 1/2 (12-ounce) package veggie burger crumbles
- 1 (8-ounce) bag vegan chicken strips
- 1/2 (12-ounce) package vegan sausage crumbles
- BBQ sauce, to taste
- Order or pick up a cheeseless pizza with your favorite veggies

Place all of the meats in a bowl and nuke until defrosted, about 30 seconds. Remove from the microwave and cut up the chicken. Add the BBQ sauce to the bowl and stir. Nuke for 2 minutes, or until hot. Dump onto the prepared pizza and chow down.

Makes 4 servings.

NOTE:

If you're lucky enough to have soy cheese at your local pizzeria, or frozen pizzas at a nearby grocery made with soy cheese, you should definitely get one of those to go with all this meat!

BIG MAN ON CAMPUS BURRITO

Busting with beans and brown rice, this is the Bigfoot of burritos. It'll make you say fee-fi-fo-yum. (It's giant, get the picture?)

1 cup microwaveable brown rice, cooked

1 (15-ounce) can black beans, drained

4 (10-inch) flour tortillas

1 cup shredded lettuce

1 (10-ounce) can diced tomatoes, drained

1/4 cup salsa

Make the rice according to the directions on the package, then set aside. Cook the beans for 30 seconds and set aside. Then heat up the tortillas for 10 seconds each or until soft. Top the tortillas with the rice, beans, lettuce, and tomatoes, then roll up and top with salsa.

Makes 4 servings.

VEGAN MAC 'N' CHEEZ

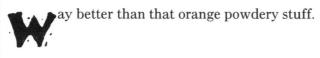**W**ay better than that orange powdery stuff.

1 (16-ounce) package elbow macaroni

1/2 cup soy milk

5 tablespoons nutritional yeast

1/2 cup vegan margarine

Salt, pepper, and garlic powder, to taste

Submerge the macaroni in water and nuke for 5 minutes; stir and repeat until completely cooked. Drain and set aside. Mix the soy milk and nutritional yeast together in the same bowl you used for the macaroni. Add the macaroni back in, along with the margarine. Mix well. If too thick, add a splash more of soy milk; if too thin, add another tablespoon of nutritional yeast. Add the salt, pepper, and garlic powder.

Makes 4 servings.

DIRTY RICE DONE DIRT CHEAP

Rice so cheap and dirty it makes Uncle Ben blush.

1 1/2 cups rice, cooked

1 1/2 (14.5-ounce) cans whole peeled tomatoes, drained

1 cup veggie burger crumbles, thawed

1 cup tomato juice

1 (4-ounce) can diced green chiles

1 teaspoon onion powder

1/2 teaspoon salt

Cook the rice according to the directions on the package, then set aside. In a bowl, combine all of the remaining ingredients. Heat in the microwave for 2 minutes, or until warm. Take out and mix in the rice. Eat.

Makes 4 servings.

NAPOLEON'S TOT CASSEROLE

You can "borrow" tater tots and green beans from the cafeteria if you need to, the same way you "borrowed" all that silverware.

- 1 (32-ounce) package frozen potato rounds
- 1 (10-ounce) package cheddar-style vegan cheese, shredded
- 1 (12-ounce) can veggie broth
- 2 tablespoons vegan sour cream
- 1 (15-ounce) can green beans, drained
- 8 slices vegan ham, torn apart
- Salt and pepper, to taste

Put the tots in a large dish and nuke for 2 minutes, or until no longer frozen. Place the shredded cheese in another bowl and nuke until it gets slightly melty. Add the broth and sour cream to the melty cheese and stir until well-mixed, then mix in the green beans and ham. Add the tots and stir until everything is mixed together. Take a serving from the bowl and put on a plate, then microwave for about 3 minutes or until hot. Repeat with remaining servings, and eat.

Makes 4 servings.

FETTUCCINE ALESSANDRO

Alfredo's vegan brother. Just as smooth, but a little cornier.

1 1/2 cups frozen corn kernels, thawed, or 1 (15-ounce)
     can corn
1 1/2 cups soy milk
1 tablespoon onion powder
1 teaspoon salt
Pepper, to taste
1 (16-ounce) package fettuccine

Place the corn, soy milk, and seasonings in a blender and process until completely smooth. It may take several minutes to completely pulverize the corn. Pour the blended mixture into a bowl and set aside. Break fettuccine in half, submerge in water and heat in the microwave for 5 minutes; stir and repeat until tender. Drain the water, put the pasta on a plate and pour the sauce over top. Heat in the microwave for another minute, or until warm. Sprinkle each portion with pepper.

Makes 4 servings.

CHICK'N NACHOS

Tortilla chips loaded like a trust fund baby.

1 (14.5-ounce) can vegetarian refried beans

2 (8-ounce) bags vegan chicken strips

1 (14.5-ounce) can diced tomatoes, drained

1/4 cup salsa

1 cup shredded lettuce

1 bag of tortilla chips

Nuke the beans and the chicken in a microwave-safe dish until hot. Add the tomatoes, salsa, and lettuce, and eat with tortilla chips.

Makes 4 servings.

"CHICKEN" AND VEGGIES

This dish will help you fight the Freshman 15 and let you grab an extra scoop of soy ice cream for dessert!

1 (10-ounce) bag microwaveable rice

1 (16-ounce) bag frozen vegetables (stir-fry mix or broccoli is best)

1 (8-ounce) bag vegan "chicken" strips

Soy sauce, to taste

Cook the rice in the microwave according to the package directions. Set aside. Cook the veggies in the microwave according to the package directions. Set aside. Cook the chicken strips in the microwave until hot, about 1 1/2 minutes. Layer the rice, veggies, and chicken in a bowl and top with soy sauce.

Makes 3 servings.

SUPER-FRAGA-MEXI-DELICIOUS RICE

Guaranteed to make you singing-to-fake-birds-and-dancing-with-cartoons kind of happy.

2 cups hot cooked rice

1 1/3 cups French-fried onions

1 cup vegan sour cream

1 (16-ounce) jar salsa

1 cup shredded cheddar-style vegan cheese

Combine the rice and 2/3 cup French-fried onions in a large bowl. Spoon half of the mixture into a large microwave-safe dish. Spread the sour cream on top. Layer half of the salsa and half of the cheese over the sour cream. Sprinkle with the remaining rice mixture, salsa, and cheese. Cover loosely with plastic wrap. Nuke for 8 minutes, or until heated through. Sprinkle with the remaining 2/3 cup onions. Nuke for 1 minute, or until the onions are golden.

Makes 4 servings.

STEAMY RISOTTO-Y GOODNESS

Missing the comforts of home after a grueling week of papers and exams? A nice steamy bowl of ricey goodness will make you feel better, even if Mom's not there to cook it for you.

3 cups hot vegetable broth

1 teaspoon onion powder

1/2 teaspoon salt

1 pinch pepper

2 tablespoons vegan margarine

2 tablespoons olive oil

1 cup uncooked instant rice

1/4 cup nutritional yeast

Combine the broth, salt, onion powder, and pepper and set aside. In a square baking dish or a glass pie plate, nuke the margarine and olive oil for 1 minute. Add the uncooked rice, stirring to coat with oil. Cover with a paper towel to prevent spattering and cook for 4 minutes. Pour the broth into the rice and stir. Nuke for 9 minutes. Stir, then cook for another 9 minutes. Remove from the microwave and immediately stir in the nutritional yeast. Serve.

Makes 4 servings.

DRINKS

Note: The following drinks are not the kind you'll find in a big metal barrel—they are the refreshing and delicious kind that won't make your head hurt the next day. Enjoy them as part of a meal, or let them stand alone in all their glory.

DID YOU KNOW?

Despite the industry's claims, the evidence is clear that the animal protein in dairy products actually pulls calcium from the body. Population studies, including a groundbreaking Harvard study of more than 75,000 nurses, suggest that drinking cow's milk actually causes osteoporosis.

FRUITY FRAT-TOOTIE SMOOTHIE

weeter than a blossoming frat boy bromance.

2–3 ripe bananas

1 (16-ounce) can pineapple chunks

1 (16-ounce) container frozen strawberries

Puree the bananas and the pineapple in a blender. Add the strawberries and mix until smooth.

Makes 4 servings.

INSTANT ENLIGHTEN-MINT CHOCOLATE LATTE

Screw finding your Zen—you need caffeine if you're going to make it to that damn 8 a.m. class.

- 1 cup chocolate soy milk
- 2–3 teaspoons instant coffee grounds
- 1/4 teaspoon peppermint extract (or 2 peppermint hard candies melted in 1/4 cup boiling water)
- Sugar, to taste

Mix all the ingredients together and nuke until hot, about 2 minutes.

Makes 1 serving.

FRUIT SMOOTHAPALOOZA

Make your own smoothies and save Mom's care package money for spring break instead!

- 1 cup soy milk
- 1 frozen banana (peel and cut into chunks before freezing)
- 1/2 cup of your favorite frozen fruit (strawberries, peaches, or pitted cherries work great)
- 1 tablespoon maple syrup

Place all the ingredients in a blender and puree until smooth.

Makes 2 servings.

NO-EGG NOG

Ho, ho—it's faux. Soy to the world! Okay, we're done.

4 cups soy milk

1 ounce instant vanilla pudding powder

1 cup nondairy whipping cream (try Rich's brand)

1 teaspoon vanilla extract

1/4 teaspoon salt

1/4 teaspoon ground nutmeg

Combine 2 cups of soy milk and the instant pudding in a medium-sized bowl, stirring until combined and thickened. Add the remaining soy milk and the nondairy whipping cream, mixing well. Stir in the vanilla, salt, and nutmeg. Refrigerate overnight.

Makes 4 servings.

MELON-BERRY BLISS

This blissful treat is not only tasty, it's chock-full of healthy fruity goodness and perfect for breakfast when you don't have time to sit down and eat properly. It's so good for you we're sure even your 'rents would approve.

- 2 frozen bananas (peeled and cut into chunks before freezing)
- 4 or 5 cantaloupe chunks (grab them from the dining hall salad bar)
- 4 or 5 honeydew chunks (grab them from the dining hall salad bar)
- 1 cup frozen blueberries
- 1 cup apple juice

Blend everything together until smooth.

Makes 2 servings.

SPRING BREAK VIRGIN SMOOTHIE

This sweet and chilly little number is just what you need to get yourself back on track after a week of spring break debauchery.

4 frozen strawberries
1 frozen banana (peel and cut into chunks before freezing)
1/4 cup orange juice

Put all the ingredients in a blender and blend until smooth. Drink.

Makes 1 serving.

NUTTY PROFESSOR ALMOND LATTE

Highly caffeinated and slightly nutty, like that frighteningly familiar professor indigenous to all anthropology departments.

1 cup almond milk

2–3 teaspoons instant coffee crystals

Sugar (optional)

Nuke the almond milk for 1 1/2 minutes. Add the instant coffee crystals, making it as strong or as weak as you'd like. Sweeten with some sugar.

Makes 1 serving.

LATE NIGHT AT THE LIBERRY SOY SMOOTHIE

Packed full of protein and potassium, it's the perfect pick-me-up after a day spent nerding around the periodicals at the library.

8 ounces soy milk

1/2 frozen banana (peeled and cut into chunks before freezing)

1 cup frozen raspberries or berry of your choice

Put all the ingredients into a blender and puree until smooth.

Makes 2 servings.

CHOCOLATE CELEBRATION SHAKE

ou've just finished your twenty-page psych paper. How will you celebrate? A chocolate shake, of course!

4 cups frozen bananas (peeled and cut into chunks before freezing)

1 cup soy milk

3 tablespoons cocoa powder

2 tablespoons maple syrup

1 teaspoon vanilla

Thaw the frozen banana chunks for 5 to 10 minutes. Toss them, and all of the other ingredients, into a blender, and puree for 2 to 3 minutes. Serve immediately.

Makes 2 servings.

PARTY IN YOUR MOUTH PUNCH

Fizzy and festive even before someone spikes it.

2 (1-quart) bottles cranberry-apple juice

1 cup brown sugar

1 (1-quart) bottle ginger ale

Orange slices, for garnish

Place the cranberry-apple juice and brown sugar in a large microwaveable dish and nuke for 3 minutes, or until the sugar is dissolved. Chill in the refrigerator for at least an hour. Before serving, combine with the ginger ale in a punch bowl. Garnish with the orange slices.

Makes 4 servings.

SUCKY DAY STRAWBERRY SHAKE

Class sucked and your friends flaked. Treat yourself to this sweet shake. You seriously deserve it.

6 strawberries

1 tablespoon sugar

2 scoops vegan ice cream

1/2 cup soy milk

Sprinkle strawberries with sugar and let sit for a minute or so. Put the ice cream, soy milk, and strawberries in a blender and blend until smooth.

Makes 2 servings.

DIPS

party just isn't a party unless someone brings the dip—or until a certain someone embarrasses himself by dancing really, really badly. Anyway, these little numbers won't leave anyone feeling bad about themselves the next day. And if you start whipping up these dips for parties, the invites you receive will quickly quadruple.

DID YOU KNOW?

Spinach grown on an acre of land can yield twenty-six times more protein than beef produced on the same acre.

PO PO'S PARTY HEARTY SPINACH DIP

You know what they say—it's not a party without dip and the cops showing up. We highly recommend that first part. The second—not so much.

- 1 (10-ounce) box frozen chopped spinach
- 1 (12-ounce) container vegan sour cream
- 1/2 cup vegan mayonnaise
- 1 packet vegan ranch dressing (McCormick's makes a vegan ranch packet) or onion soup mix
- 1 round loaf sourdough bread or other round loaf

Thaw the spinach in a bowl in the microwave for about 40 seconds on high. Using your hands, squeeze out all the water. Put the spinach in a dry bowl and stir in the sour cream, mayonnaise, and packet of ranch dressing/onion soup mix. Let sit for a couple of hours, allowing the flavors to blend. Cut the top off the bread and scoop out the middle, making a bowl. Serve the dip in the bread bowl and cut the bread you scooped out into chunks for dipping.

Makes 8 servings.

FREUDIAN DIP

A therapeutic blend of beans, vegan sour cream, and salsa. Guaranteed to solve even the biggest of edible complexes.

1 (15.5-ounce) can vegetarian refried beans

1 (12-ounce) container of vegan sour cream

1 (16-ounce) jar salsa

Jalapeños, sliced, to taste

Tortilla chips

Mix all the ingredients, except the chips, together in a bowl and nuke for 2 minutes, or until warm. Serve with tortilla chips.

Makes 8 servings.

CRAB-ULOUS DIP

Dive in—this flavorful faux crab dip is the closest you'll ever get to a semester at sea.

1 (12-ounce) can artichoke hearts, drained

12 ounces firm tofu, drained, patted dry, and broken up

1/2 cup vegan mayonnaise

Old Bay seasoning

Crackers

Chop the artichoke hearts and place in a bowl. Add the tofu, mayonnaise, and approximately 1 tablespoon of Old Bay. Nuke for 1 1/2 minutes, checking to see if the top is slightly bubbly. If it's not, nuke for another 1 1/2 minutes. Top with another sprinkle of Old Bay and serve warm with crackers.

Makes 8 servings.

SPIN ART DIP

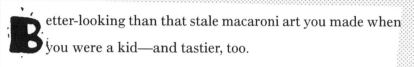

Better-looking than that stale macaroni art you made when you were a kid—and tastier, too.

1/2 (10-ounce) package frozen chopped spinach

1 (15-ounce) jar marinated artichoke hearts (drained but not rinsed)

1 teaspoon garlic powder

1 cup vegan mayonnaise

1/2 cup nutritional yeast (you can use vegan parmesan cheese as well)

Pepper, to taste

1 bag of bagel chips

Defrost the spinach in the microwave by heating for about 40 seconds on high power, then squeeze out the excess water. Chop up the artichoke hearts. Mix all the ingredients, except for the bagel chips, together in a bowl. Nuke for 3 minutes, or until bubbly. Serve with bagel chips—and try not to eat all the dip yourself.

Makes 8 servings.

MEXI-CRAM DIP

Scare up some tortilla chips and you've got the perfect snack for getting your learn on lightning fast.

1 (15-ounce) can vegan chili or 2 cups homemade vegan chili

1 (8-ounce) container vegan cream cheese

1 (4.25-ounce) can sliced black olives

1 package taco seasoning

Jalapeño slices, to taste

Mix the ingredients together in a bowl and nuke for 1 minute, or until warm.

Makes 8 servings.

DARWIN'S DIP

A natural selection for that party you're planning. Do a couple of lunges though—it's all about survival of the fittest once this delish black bean dip hits the table.

1 (15-ounce) can black beans, drained and rinsed

1 cup salsa

1 tablespoon lemon juice (fresh or via squirt bottle)

1 teaspoon onion powder

Mash beans with a fork. Add the salsa, lemon juice, and onion powder. Stir well and refrigerate before serving.

Makes 8 servings.

SEVEN-LAYER MEXICAN DIP

Layer upon layer of deliciousness. This dip is deeper than most of your friends.

- 1 (8-ounce) package vegan cream cheese
- 1 tablespoon taco seasoning mix
- 1 (15.5-ounce) can vegetarian refried beans
- 1 cup guacamole (see page 218)
- 1 cup chunky salsa
- 1 cup shredded lettuce
- 1 cup shredded soy cheddar cheese
- 2 tablespoons dried chives
- 1 small can sliced black olives

Mix the cream cheese and taco seasoning together. Spread onto the bottom of a 9-inch pie plate or other dish. Layer the beans, guacamole, salsa, lettuce, cheese, chives, and olives over the cream cheese mixture. Cover and refrigerate for a least 1 hour. Serve with tortilla chips.

Makes 8 servings.

CHOW DOWN CHILI-"CHEESE" DIP

This "cheesy," spicy dip goes great with corn chips and will have even the biggest meathead on campus coming back for more.

1 (15-ounce) can vegan chili or 2 cups prepared vegan chili
1 tablespoon Mrs. Dash seasoning
2 slices vegan cheese
1 tablespoon black pepper
1 bag Fritos

Put the chili, Mrs. Dash, cheese, and black pepper into a big bowl and nuke for 2 minutes. Stir, then use Fritos for scooping.

Makes 8 servings.

CAMPUS STREAKER SAUSAGE DIP

reat for when you're on the run. Guaranteed to turn any party into a sausage fest.

- 1 (14-ounce) tube vegan sausage
- 2 (8-ounce) containers of vegan cream cheese, room temperature
- 1 (15-ounce) can diced tomatoes with mild green chiles, undrained

Crumble the sausage as best you can and stir it into the cream cheese and tomatoes until evenly blended. Heat in the microwave for 3 minutes, or until hot. Serve with tortilla chips.

Makes 8 servings.

CHEEZY BREEZY BEAN DIP

Because you know that dried-up tray of nacho dip stuff in the cafeteria has been there since, like, 1992.

- 1 (14.5-ounce) can vegetarian refried beans
- 1 (8-ounce) can diced chiles
- 1/3 package vegan cheese, grated

Put all the ingredients in a bowl, cover, and cook for about 2 minutes. Remove from the microwave and stir. Nuke for another minute or two. Stir again before serving with your fave chips.

Makes 8 servings.

UNHOLY GUACAMOLE

If the devil had a dip, this would be it.

3 large avocados, cut in half and pits removed

1/4 cup chopped cilantro

1 (16-ounce) jar salsa

Salt, to taste

Scoop the avocado flesh into a bowl. Add the cilantro and salsa, and mix it all together. Season with salt and eat. Serve with chips, on top of nachos, in burritos, or by itself.

Makes 8 servings.

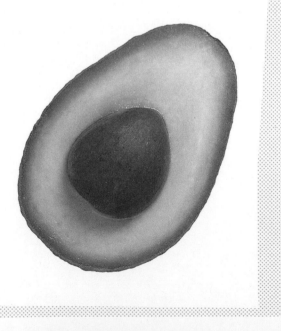

FLOOR PARTY FOUR-LAYER BEAN DIP

Make up for your bad taste in late night study music by charming your fellow dorm-dwellers with an example of your good taste in food.

1 (15.5-ounce) can refried beans
1 (12-ounce) container guacamole
1 (8-ounce) can diced tomatoes
1 (4.25-ounce) can chopped black olives
Black pepper, to taste
1 bag tortilla chips

Spread the can of beans on a large plate and nuke till warm. Top with the guac, then the tomatoes, and then the olives. Sprinkle with some pepper and serve with chips!

Makes 8 servings.

CRAZY GUAC-ODILE DIP

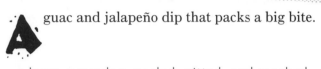

A guac and jalapeño dip that packs a big bite.

3 large avocados, peeled, pitted, and mashed

1 (14.5-ounce) can diced tomatoes, drained

2 tablespoons dried cilantro (optional)

1 tablespoon chopped jalapeños (canned is okay)

1 teaspoon onion powder

Salt, to taste

Mix everything together and serve with chips or in tacos, burritos, etc.

Makes 8 servings.

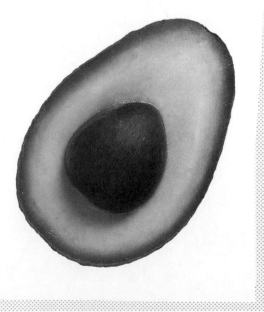

ORANGU-TANGY ORANGE SPREAD

This sweet spread gets two opposable thumbs up.

1 (8-ounce) container vegan cream cheese, softened
1 (10-ounce) jar orange marmalade
Crackers

Mix the vegan cream cheese with the orange marmalade in a bowl until well combined. Serve with crackers.

Makes 8 servings.

WOWY MAUI TROPICAL FRUIT SPREAD

This creamy coco-pine-orange concoction is hanging five in Hawaii, getting lei'd, and busting out the ukulele.

1/2 (8-ounce) container vegan cream cheese

1/2 cup vegan sour cream

1 (8-ounce) can crushed pineapple, drained

1/2 cup canned mandarin oranges, drained

1 tablespoon coconut flakes (optional)

Mix everything together until well blended. Serve with crackers.

Makes 8 servings.

CHILLY DILLY SKINNY DIP

Great served with veggies *and* vegetarians in the raw. So close your drawers and hope that the only thing chilly is the dip.

- 1 cup vegan mayonnaise
- 1 (12-ounce) container vegan sour cream
- 1 1/2 teaspoons dill weed
- 1 teaspoon salt
- 1 teaspoon onion powder
- 1 teaspoon garlic powder

Stir everything together in a bowl and let chill in the refrigerator for at least one hour. Serve with raw veggies or potato chips.

Makes 8 servings.

FIESTA IN YOUR MOUTH SALSA

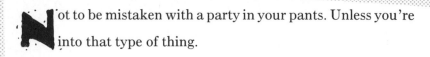ot to be mistaken with a party in your pants. Unless you're into that type of thing.

- 1 (28-ounce) can diced tomatoes, drained
- 1 (8-ounce) can diced green chiles, drained
- 1 (4.25-ounce) can diced black olives, drained
- 1/4 cup olive oil
- 1/4 cup distilled white vinegar
- 1 tablespoon dried chives
- 2 teaspoons garlic powder
- Salt, to taste

Mix all the ingredients together in a bowl and place in the fridge to chill for at least 1 hour. Stir before serving with corn tortilla chips.

Makes 8 servings.

DORM ROOM 'SHROOM DIP

Tight quarters, tight budget, tight dip.

1/2 pound fresh mushrooms, sliced

2 1/2 tablespoons vegetable oil

1 teaspoon garlic powder

1 package vegan onion soup mix

1/8 teaspoon pepper

1 (8-ounce) container vegan cream cheese, softened

8 ounces vegan sour cream

2 tablespoons vegan bacon bits

Crackers or small chunks of rye bread

Combine the mushrooms, oil, and garlic powder in a bowl and nuke, uncovered, for 2 minutes or until the mushrooms are tender, stirring once. Add the soup mix, pepper, and cream cheese, and stir together thoroughly. Nuke again, uncovered, for 3 minutes, stirring frequently. Stir in the sour cream and the bacon bits. Nuke, uncovered, for 3 minutes, or until heated through, stirring once. Serve with crackers or rye bread.

Makes 8 servings.

SPRING BREAK TAHINI BIKINI DIP

Getting baked by the sun and playing in the ocean all day can really take a lot out of you. After a day at the beach the last thing you want to do is cook, so munch on this delicious dip instead.

1 cup tahini
1 cup salsa
Tortilla chips

Mix the salsa and tahini together in a serving bowl. Serve with tortilla chips.

Makes 8 servings.

NACHO MOMMA'S CHEEZ DIP

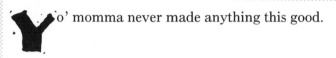o' momma never made anything this good.

- 1 (10-ounce) package vegan nacho-style cheese
- 1 (16-ounce) container salsa
- 1 (12-ounce) container vegan sour cream
- 1(12-ounce) bag veggie burger crumbles

Mix everything together in a bowl and nuke for 5 minutes, or until the crumbles are warm and the cheese is melted. Serve with tortilla chips.

Makes 8 servings.

SALSA FOR BEGINNERS

Way easier than trying to con your boyfriend into taking salsa lessons with you, and cheaper, too.

3 tablespoons vegan cream cheese

1 cup salsa

Mix the ingredients together and enjoy. Serve with tortilla chips.

Makes 4 servings.

"WALK OF SHAME" SUGAR DIP

Hold your head up; we've all done some pretty stupid things to get some sugar. Unlike last night, this sweet dip won't leave you with regrets *or* a bad reputation.

1 (8-ounce) container vegan cream cheese

3/4 cup brown sugar

1/4 cup white sugar

2 teaspoons vanilla

1/2 cup dry-roasted peanuts (optional)

Apple slices

Using a hand mixer, beat the vegan cream cheese, sugars, and vanilla. If you don't have a hand mixer, use your blender, but cut the cream cheese into small pieces first. Stir in the nuts, if using. Serve with the apple slices.

Makes 8 servings.

CHEATER'S CHEESECAKE DIP

Cheating on tests? Bad idea. Pulling a fast one on your friends with this recipe? Great idea! They'll never know.

2 cups vegan marshmallow cream (Smucker's and Ricemellow are good vegan options)
1 (8-ounce) container vegan cream cheese, softened

Cream the ingredients together by mixing together slowly, then refrigerate for a while. Serve with fruit from the cafeteria's salad bar.

Makes 8 servings.

BROWN SUGAR FUN DIP

Remember those "Fun Dip" packs from when you were a kid? You know, the peppermint stick you'd dip into that crack-cocaine-like powder and lick until your head throbbed from the sugar? Well, think of this as Fun Dip's older, healthier cousin.

- 1 (8-ounce) container vegan cream cheese
- 2 tablespoons brown sugar

Stir together and serve with fresh fruit.

Makes 4 servings.

FEISTY FRUIT SALSA

Part sweet, part hot, just like your latest online crush.

1 (16-ounce) tub pre-cut fruit of your choice

1 teaspoon chopped chives

1 tablespoon chopped fresh jalapeños (or use canned)

1 tablespoon lime juice (fresh or from a squirt bottle)

Put all the ingredients into a bowl and mix well. Cover and chill for several hours or overnight.

Makes 4 servings

NOTE:

If you have a toaster oven, make chips to serve with the fruit salsa by brushing flour tortillas with melted vegan margarine, then sprinkling with a mixture of cinnamon and sugar. Cut into wedges, and bake at 350°F until crispy.

SNACKS

Feel like a treat? Is your stomach growling so loudly you can hear it over your iPod? Or do you just want to impress the people that keep wandering in and out of your room? These snacks are perfect for all those occasions, as well as between classes, on a study break, or late at night, when you're watching *Animal House* for the tenth time. They're fast, convenient, and have been known to help you miraculously make new friends with people down the hall, or even on different floors. You know what we mean—all of a sudden everyone is your best friend when you have tasty-looking food.

DID YOU KNOW?

As a vegetarian, your bones will last longer. The average bone loss for a vegetarian woman at age 65 is 18 percent; for non-vegetarian women, it's double that.

SHAM "HAM" ROLL-UPS

You've always wanted to make something with chives because they sound fancy—admit it.

1 (8-ounce) container vegan cream cheese

1 tablespoon chopped chives

Salt and pepper, to taste

1 (5.5-ounce) package vegan ham deli slices

Mix the cream cheese, chives, salt, and pepper together. Spread the mixture on the deli slices and roll up. Use a toothpick to hold together.

Makes 4 servings.

UNDERCOVER OINKERS

These "pigs in a blanket" aren't really pigs at all, but we won't tell if you won't.

1 (12-ounce) package vegan hot dogs
Vegan cheese slices (optional)
1 (9-ounce) package vegan crescent rolls
Your choice of condiments

Roll the hot dogs (and cheese, if using) up in the crescent rolls. Oil a plate so the rolls won't stick to it, then place the rolls on the plate and heat in the microwave for 10 minutes, or until fluffy.

Makes 4 servings.

SLACKER SLAW

If you're too lazy to make this super-easy slaw, we need to have a talk with your parents.

1/2 (16-ounce) bag coleslaw mix

1 tablespoon chopped chives

2 tablespoons diced celery (visit your local salad bad if you don't feel like dicing)

1/4 cup vegan mayonnaise

2 teaspoons lemon juice (use fresh or from the squirt bottle)

Salt and pepper, to taste

Toss together the coleslaw mix, chives, and celery in a large bowl. Add the mayonnaise and lemon juice, and stir. Refrigerate for at least 30 minutes before serving.

Makes 4 servings.

CHILI "NOT" DOGS

Bring these wieners to your next sausage—er, soysage—party and watch 'em disappear.

1 vegan hot dog

1 hot dog bun

1/4 cup vegan chili or prepared vegan chili

Mustard

Dill relish (optional)

Cook the hot dog according to the package directions. Place in the bun and top with the chili, mustard, and dill relish. Serve with onion rings or French fries.

Makes 1 serving.

ONE-BITE PIZZAS

Downing an entire beer in one breath? Big deal. Now you can brag to your buddies that you can take out a whole pizza in one bite.

- 1/2 (12-ounce) bag veggie burger crumbles
- 1/2 (14-ounce) tube vegan sausage
- 1 (14-ounce) jar pizza sauce or any other tomato sauce
- 4 slices vegan cheese, cut into quarters
- 1 bag mini bagels, toasted

Mix the crumbles and sausage together and nuke for 2 to 3 minutes, or until warm. Take out of the microwave and mix in the pizza sauce. Spoon onto the bagels, top with 1/4 of a slice of cheese, and nuke for 20 seconds, or until the cheese is melted.

Makes 4 servings.

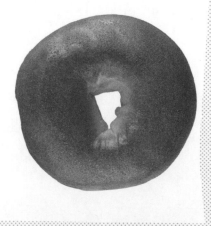

OYSTER CRACKER SNACKERS

So good you can't just have one...

3/4 cup olive oil

1/2 teaspoon garlic powder

1/2 teaspoon onion powder

1 teaspoon salt

1 (24-ounce) bag oyster crackers

Additional onion powder and garlic powder, to taste

Mix the oil, garlic powder, onion powder, and salt together in a small bowl. Place the crackers on a baking sheet with a lip and pour the oil mixture over the crackers, sprinkling them with more garlic powder and onion powder. Let sit for 10 minutes, mix, then let sit for an additional 20 minutes. Mix again and eat.

Makes 4 servings.

NERDY BIRDY CHICK'N BYTES

Fake chicken for peeps who spend most of their time in a fake world. Hearty enough for hard-core gamers and enough to feed an entire army of avatars.

1 package taco seasoning
1 tablespoon vegan mayonnaise
1 (8-ounce) package vegan chicken strips
Salsa

Mix the taco seasoning with the mayonnaise. Put the mixture in a large resealable bag and add the chicken. Shake the bag like crazy to coat the chicken. Remove from the bag, put on a plate, and nuke for 1 minute. Dip in salsa.

Makes 4 servings.

SHUCKIN' AWESOME CORN ON THE COB

A delicious meal and if you're feeling crafty, a chance to be the only guy on campus rocking a corncob pipe. Everyone knows that ladies can't resist a corncob pipe. How do you think Mark Twain got so much tail?

4 ears of corn, still in the husk
Salt, pepper, and vegan margarine, to taste

Pop two of the ears of corn in the microwave and nuke for 8 minutes. Take the corn out of the microwave with your oven mitts or other hand-protecting device and shuck the corn. Repeat with the other two ears of corn. Put the shucked corn on a plate and top with salt, pepper, and margarine, or just eat it plain.

Makes 4 servings.

LEMONY CARROTS

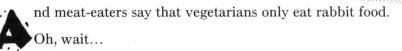

And meat-eaters say that vegetarians only eat rabbit food. Oh, wait…

1/2 (10-ounce) bag baby carrots

1 tablespoon vegan margarine

1 tablespoon lemon juice, or more to taste

Salt and pepper, to taste

Arrange the carrots in a single layer on a plate and dot with margarine. Cover and nuke for 6 minutes, or until almost tender. Sprinkle with lemon juice and season with salt and pepper.

Makes 4 servings.

POOR MAN'S PIZZAS

Ivy-league eating on a community-college budget.

  24 crackers of your choice

  1/4 cup pizza sauce

  24 slices vegan pepperoni or other "meat" topping of your
    choice

  1 1/2 cups finely shredded mozzarella-style vegan cheese

Top each cracker with some pizza sauce, pepperoni or other meat, and vegan cheese. Microwave for 1 minute, or until the "cheese" is melted.

Makes 4 servings.

HAPPY TRAILZ MIX

reat for grazing a trail across campus.

1/2 cup corn-puff cereal (try Corn Pops or Kix)

1/2 cup mixed nuts

1/4 cup mini pretzels

1/4 cup dried pineapple

1/4 cup raisins

1 vegan chocolate bar, broken apart

1/4 cup coconut flakes (optional)

Mix all the ingredients together.

Makes 4 servings.

THE "I MISS MY MOMMY" SPECIAL

Homesick roomie? Show the poor chump some love with 'this home-style favorite—but also remind him that you'll have to ground him if he doesn't start acting like a "big boy."

- 2 (14.5-ounce) cans French-style green beans, drained
- 1 (2.8-ounce can) French-fried onions
- 3 tablespoons nutritional yeast
- 1 tablespoon vegetarian chicken-style broth powder (try Imagine's No-Chicken Broth)
- 1 teaspoon garlic powder
- Salt, to taste

Combine all of the ingredients and put into a microwave-safe bowl. Nuke for 3 minutes or until hot. Eat.

Makes 4 servings.

PIZZA FUN-DO

Totally do-able cheezy fondue that will leave your friends swooning.

1 (12-ounce) bag veggie burger crumbles

1 teaspoon onion powder

1 teaspoon garlic powder

2 (10-ounce) cans pizza sauce

3 cups vegan cheese, shredded

Cubed French bread

Mix the crumbles with the onion and garlic powders and nuke until warm, about 1 minute. Mix in the remaining ingredients, except the bread. Nuke, uncovered, for 12 to 14 minutes, until the cheese melts. Stir to blend. Serve with bread cubes to dip into the fondue.

Makes 4 servings.

CAULI-FLOWER POWER FLORETS

D·ig that Dijon.

1 (14-ounce) bag frozen cauliflower florets

1/2 cup vegan mayonnaise

1/4 cup Dijon mustard

1 cup shredded cheddar-style vegan cheese

Place the cauliflower in a bowl and nuke for 5 minutes, or until warm. Remove from the microwave. In another bowl, mix the mayonnaise and the mustard. Spoon onto the cauliflower and top with the cheese. Nuke for an additional 2 minutes, or until the cheese is melted.

Makes 4 servings.

PANCAKE PIZZA

You already start the day at the crack of noon; you might as well combine lunch with breakfast, too.

1 cup vegan pancake mix

1/2 cup soy milk

1 1/2 teaspoons egg replacer mixed with 2 tablespoons water

1/2 (8-ounce) can mushrooms, pieces and stems

1/2 (8-ounce) can black olives, sliced

1/2 cup shredded vegan cheese

Pizza sauce, to taste

In a small bowl, mix together the pancake mix, soy milk, and egg replacer/water mixture. Stir until blended. Add the mushrooms, olives, and cheese. Microwave for 2 minutes, or until solid. Top with pizza sauce and enjoy.

Makes 1 serving.

STADIUM CORN DOGS

Feel free to put these on a stick to get the experience of the game from the comfort of your room.

1 cup cornmeal

1 cup all-purpose flour (unbleached)

1 tablespoon baking powder

1 teaspoon salt

1/3 cup canola oil

1 cup soy milk

1 teaspoon egg replacer mixed with 1/4 cup of water

4 veggie dogs, sliced

Ketchup and mustard, for dipping

Put dry ingredients (except the hot dogs) in one bowl and mix; put the wet ingredients in another bowl and mix. Combine the wet and dry ingredients into a square casserole dish and mix until smooth. Plop the hot dogs in the mixture equal distance apart and pop in the microwave. Nuke on high for 5 minutes or until surface appears dry, rotating bowl after 2–3 minutes. Let stand 5 minutes before serving. Cut into squares and serve with ketchup and mustard for dipping.

Makes 4 servings.

NO-PAN CROUTONS

Delicious with salad or on their own, and way better than those crusty little bricks they serve at the caf.

1/4 cup vegan margarine

2 teaspoons garlic powder

1 teaspoon salt

4 cups French bread, cut into 3/4-inch cubes

Place the margarine in a bowl and nuke for 1 minute, or until melted. Stir in the garlic and salt. Add the bread cubes, stirring gently to coat. Place in a bowl and microwave on high for 4 1/2 to 5 minutes, stirring 2 or 3 times. Let cool. Store in an airtight container. (The croutons will crisp as they cool.)

Makes 4 servings.

GRANDMA'S HOMEMADE APPLESAUCE

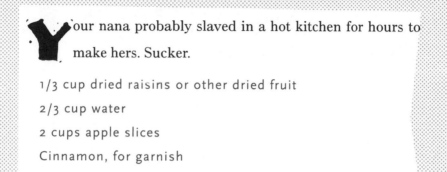

Your nana probably slaved in a hot kitchen for hours to make hers. Sucker.

1/3 cup dried raisins or other dried fruit

2/3 cup water

2 cups apple slices

Cinnamon, for garnish

Place dried fruit in a bowl, cover with some water, and let sit for 15 minutes. Drain and place them in a blender with the apple slices and puree. Top with some cinnamon before serving.

Makes 4 servings.

SLAYER'S SLICE

One taste, and you can ward off any campus vampires simply by breathing on them.

Rolls of any kind, cut in half (hamburger buns, hot dog buns, dinner rolls, etc.), toasted

Olive oil

Garlic salt

Dried oregano or parsley, if you have it

Brush the sliced side of the bread with a little olive oil (you don't want to soak it, but make sure the surface is covered). Sprinkle with a little garlic salt and dried oregano or parsley, if using. Nuke in a microwave for 15 seconds.

Makes 4 servings.

GODDESS OF THE GARBANZOS

You'll become an empowered empress and be ready to take on the world once this dish touches your taste buds.

1 (15-ounce) can chickpeas, drained
1/4 cup Annie's Goddess Dressing

Mix together the dressing and chickpeas in a bowl and eat.

Makes 2 servings.

EXTRA CREDIT "HAM" TOAST POINTS

0% effort; 110% *satisfacción.*

  2 (5.5-ounce) packages vegan ham deli slices

  3 cups vegan mayonnaise

  1 cup soy parmesan cheese

  1 cup shredded or diced vegan cheddar cheese

  2 teaspoons garlic powder

  1 teaspoon onion powder

  2 large loaves Italian bread

Tear apart the slices of ham, then combine them in a bowl with the mayo, cheeses, garlic powder, and onion powder. Slice and toast the bread; when toasted, top with a spoonful of the spread. Pop them in the microwave until the cheese is melted.

Makes 8 servings.

FRANKIE'S FARTS

Not a good meal to eat before a date, an exam, or pretty much any situation where others will be trapped in close proximity to you, but delicious nonetheless! Our apologies to your roommate.

1 (15.5-ounce) can vegetarian baked beans
1 package vegan hot dogs

Open the can of beans and pour into a microwave-safe bowl. Slice or tear apart however many veggie dogs you would like to use and place in the same bowl. Nuke for 3 minutes and eat.

Makes 4 servings.

GOLIVE HARDEN BRUSCHETTA

Like the fancy stuff at that Italian place, without the crying babies and jacked-up prices.

1 (14.5-ounce) can diced tomatoes, drained

1 (2.25-ounce) can chopped black olives, drained

2 tablespoons olive oil

2 teaspoons balsamic vinegar (or less for a milder flavor)

Garlic powder, to taste

Salt and pepper, to taste

1 whole-wheat pita

Put the tomatoes and olives in a bowl and mix together. Add the olive oil and balsamic vinegar and stir, mixing well. Season with garlic powder, salt, and pepper. Toast the pita in toaster. Tear into smaller pieces. Dip into the tomato mixture, scooping some of the olives and tomatoes, and eat!

Makes 2 servings.

EZ CHEEZY BROCCOLEEZY

No, nutritional yeast is not a malady caused by malnutrition. It's a delicious cheese alternative best when served smothered on broccoli. 'Nuff said.

1 (10-ounce) bag frozen broccoli florets
1/4 cup nutritional yeast
Salt, to taste
2 tablespoons margarine

Nuke the broccoli for 4 minutes. Set aside. Mix the salt and nutritional yeast together and sprinkle onto the broccoli. Add the margarine and nuke for 1 minute. Stir together and eat!

Makes 2 servings.

DON'T GET CREAMED SPINACH

Let's face it, that inadvertent bicep curl you do when you bring your fork to your mouth is as close as you're going to get to pumping iron. Better load up on as much spinach as you can.

3/4 cup soy milk

2 tablespoons vegan margarine

2 tablespoons flour

1/4 teaspoon salt

Pepper, to taste

1 (10-ounce) package frozen spinach, thawed

Heat everything but the spinach together in the microwave for 30 seconds. Stir. Heat again for 30 seconds. Stir again. Add the thawed spinach and nuke for 1 minute. Stir and eat.

Makes 2 servings.

"AGE OF ASPARAGUS" SPEARS

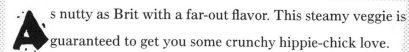

As nutty as Brit with a far-out flavor. This steamy veggie is guaranteed to get you some crunchy hippie-chick love.

1/2 pound fresh asparagus, woody ends trimmed or snapped off

2 teaspoons red wine vinegar

3–4 tablespoons olive oil

Salt and black pepper, to taste

Chopped walnuts

Nuke the asparagus for 2 to 3 minutes, until crisp but tender. While it's cooking, whisk together the vinegar, oil, salt, and pepper. To serve, drizzle the vinaigrette over the asparagus and garnish with the chopped walnuts.

Makes 2 servings.

BOOZY BEER BREAD

The bad news is that it won't slide through your beer bong. The good news is you can seriously eat about twenty loaves of this beer-soaked bread before someone wrestles your car keys from you.

2 cups self-rising flour

1 cup all-purpose flour

3 tablespoons sugar

12 ounces beer, at room temperature

Cooking spray, to coat

Cornflake crumbs, to taste

1 tablespoon vegan margarine, softened

Mix flours, sugar, and beer together to make your batter. Spray a glass loaf pan with cooking spray, then sprinkle the bottom and sides with crumbs. Spoon batter into pan and top with margarine, making sure top is evenly coated. Then add a light sprinkling of cornflake crumbs. Nuke on medium heat for 9 minutes, then on high heat for 2 minutes.

Makes 4 servings.

FANCY PANTS GREEN BEANS

Spicy as an Argentine salsa on that TV dance show you'll never admit you like, but much more appetizing then the "manitards" the contestants wear.

1 (15-ounce) can fancy sliced green beans, drained
1 tablespoon vegan margarine
1 tablespoon salsa
1/2 teaspoon spicy sesame oil

Mix everything together in a bowl and nuke for about 1 1/2 minutes, until hot.

Makes 4 servings.

FRIENDS WITH BENNIES BAKED BEANS

An easy and fulfilling recipe you don't have to commit a lot of time or energy to. And much like that FWB thing you got going on, these beans may come back later to bite you in the ass.

1 (16-ounce) can baked beans, undrained
1 (16-ounce) can red kidney beans, drained
1/2 cup chunky style prepared salsa
1 teaspoon onion powder
1 teaspoon prepared mustard

Combine all the ingredients in a bowl and mix well. Cover with microwave-safe wax paper and nuke for 7 to 9 1/2 minutes, or until the flavors are blended, stirring twice during cooking.

Makes 4 servings.

MUY CALIENTE CORN

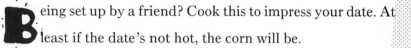

Being set up by a friend? Cook this to impress your date. At least if the date's not hot, the corn will be.

1 (14-ounce) can corn, drained

1 (7-ounce) can diced jalapeños, drained

1 teaspoon onion powder

1 (4-ounce) jar pimentos

2 tablespoons vegan margarine

Salt and pepper, to taste

Combine the corn, jalapeños, onion powder, pimentos, and margarine in a microwave-safe bowl. Cover and nuke for 4 minutes or until hot, stirring every minute or so. Add salt and pepper and eat.

Makes 4 servings.

TROPICAL LOVE TRIANGLES

Polynesian-inspired toaster points as sweet and satisfying as any tropical delight you can imagine, but without any of the travel hassles.

- 8 slices of your favorite bread
- 1 (15-ounce) can tomato sauce
- 1 (14-ounce) can pineapple, crushed and drained
- 1 box vegan baked ham deli slices
- 1 package mozzarella-style vegan cheese (Tofutti melts the best in this case)

Cut crusts off bread. Toast the bread and cut each piece in half diagonally so you have two triangles. Take the bread out of the toaster and spread the tomato sauce on each slice. Tear up a slice of ham and place on top of the toast, then sprinkle the pineapple on the toast and top with vegan cheese. Repeat process for each piece of toast. Pop in the microwave for 30 seconds or until cheese is melted.

Makes 4 servings.

STUFFED DORM ROOM 'SHROOMS

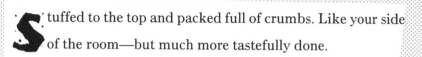

Stuffed to the top and packed full of crumbs. Like your side of the room—but much more tastefully done.

1/2 pound medium-size mushrooms, washed, with stems removed and saved

4 tablespoons vegan margarine

1/2 cup chopped chives

3 tablespoons breadcrumbs

Arrange the mushroom caps, hollow side up, in a single layer in a baking dish. Set aside. Chop up the mushroom stems and combine with the margarine and chives in another dish. Nuke, uncovered, for 3 to 4 minutes, stirring twice. Add the breadcrumbs, stir, and set aside. Cover the mushroom caps and nuke for 2 to 3 minutes, or until nearly cooked, rotating the dish a half turn after the first minute. Stuff each cap with some of the breadcrumb mixture. Cover and nuke for 2 minutes, or until hot.

Makes 4 servings.

NO "DOUGH" PIZZA

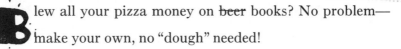

Blew all your pizza money on ~~beer~~ books? No problem—
make your own, no "dough" needed!

1 slice bread

Spaghetti sauce, to taste

1 slice vegan cheese

4 slices vegan pepperoni

Toast the bread in the toaster. Take out and top with the sauce,
cheese, and pepperoni. Place in microwave and nuke until the
cheese is melted.

Makes 1 serving.

LIMON SPINACH

It's like the liquor: tasty, fresh, and delicious, except you can't get arrested for carrying this in an open container.

2 (10-ounce) bags pre-washed fresh spinach, rinsed

5 tablespoons vegan margarine

2 tablespoons lemon juice (fresh or from squirt bottle)

2 teaspoons garlic powder

Salt and pepper to taste

Put the spinach in a serving dish. Add the margarine, garlic, and lemon juice. Cover with plastic wrap. Nuke for about 2 minutes, or until the margarine is melted and the spinach is wilted. Remove the plastic wrap and eat.

Makes 4 servings.

SPOTLIGHT ON: POTATOES

There are thousands of varieties of potatoes and just as many ways to prepare them. This is definitely a good thing, since potatoes are delicious and filling. They're also a great defense weapon (who would ever expect you to throw a potato at them?)—but that's beside the point. Potatoes are quick, tasty, and easy to make so be sure to always keep some on hand.

DID YOU KNOW?

Raising animals for food requires massive amounts of food and raw materials: Farmed animals consume 70 percent of the corn, wheat, and other grains that we grow, and one-third of all the raw materials and fossil fuels used in the U.S. go to raising animals for food.

GERMAN 'TATO SALAD

Even if you can't get to the beer garden, you can be an honorary German year-round with this tasty concoction of 'taters and mustard.

2 lbs. red potatoes

1/2 cup chopped chives

1 cup vegan bacon bits

6 tablespoons vinegar, or to taste

1/3 cup vegetable oil

3 tablespoons brown mustard, or to taste

Salt and pepper, to taste

Wash the potatoes and stab them with a fork (to vent). Place in microwave for 5 minutes or until tender. You should be able to easily stick a fork in them, but they shouldn't fall apart. Cut into cubes. In a large bowl, mix together the bacon bits, chives, vinegar, oil, and mustard. Toss the potatoes into the bowl and mix until the potatoes are well-coated. Add salt and pepper.

Makes 4 servings.

CLASSIC POTATO SALAD FAKE-OUT

With vegan mayo instead of the eggy original, no one will ever guess that their new favorite classic potato salad is a faker.

4 large russet or Idaho potatoes

1 cup vegan mayonnaise

1 teaspoon Dijon mustard

1 cup chopped celery

1/2 cup chopped chives

Salt and pepper, to taste

Wash the potatoes and stab them with a fork (to vent). Place in microwave for 8 minutes or until tender. You should be able to stick a fork in them, but they shouldn't fall apart. Cut into cubes. In a large bowl, mix together the mayonnaise, mustard, celery, and chives. Add the potatoes and toss until well coated. Add salt and pepper. Chill and serve.

Makes 4 servings.

TOUGH AND STUFFED SWEET POTATOES

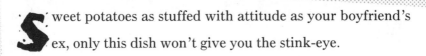weet potatoes as stuffed with attitude as your boyfriend's ex, only this dish won't give you the stink-eye.

4 medium sweet potatoes

1 (15-ounce) can black beans, drained

1 (10-ounce) can diced tomatoes

1 tablespoon vegetable oil

3/4 teaspoon salt

1/4 cup vegan sour cream

Stab the sweet potatoes with a fork in several places to vent. Nuke until tender all the way to the center, 12 to 15 minutes. Meanwhile, in a medium bowl, mix together the beans, tomatoes, oil, and salt. Nuke for about 2 to 3 minutes, until just heated through. When just cool enough to handle, cut each sweet potato lengthwise (being careful not to cut all the way through), press open to make a well in the center, and spoon the bean mixture into the well. Top with some sour cream.

Makes 4 servings.

TEACHER'S PET TATER SKINS

Lay it on thick and hang on every bite. We promise, the Bac-Os are as Fake-O as your interest in what the teacher is actually saying.

1 potato
2 slices vegan cheese
1 tablespoon vegan bacon bits
2 tablespoons vegan sour cream
Salt and pepper, to taste

Stab the potato with a fork multiple times, like a blonde in a bad horror flick. Nuke on high for 5 minutes, or until tender. Take out of the microwave and cut in half. Top with the cheese and bacon bits. Place back in the microwave and nuke for another minute. Take out and top with the sour cream, salt, and pepper.

Makes 1 serving.

THE SWEETNESS 'TATER SALAD

Next to bringing a cooler full of "refreshing beverages," bringing this surprisingly sweet 'tater salad to your next picnic is the easiest way to score points with your pals.

1 sweet potato, peeled and grated

1 (16-ounce) bag coleslaw mix (shredded cabbage)

1/2 (10-ounce) bag shredded carrots

Handful of raisins

1 apple, cored and diced

1/2 (20-ounce) can diced pineapple, do not drain

1/4 cup lemon juice

1/4 cup olive oil

Toss all the ingredients together in a large bowl and serve immediately.

Makes 2 servings.

PIONEER POTATO SALAD

Tastes like your 100-year-old granny's 200-year-old recipe.

2–3 medium potatoes (try to pick ones around the same size for even cooking), washed

1/2 cup vegan mayonnaise

2 teaspoons garlic powder

1 teaspoon pepper

Dill relish, to taste

Stab the potatoes with a fork (to vent) and nuke for about 3 minutes. Flip the potatoes over (careful, they're hot!) and nuke for another 3 minutes. Mix the mayo, spices, and relish in a medium-sized bowl. Let the potatoes rest in the microwave for a few minutes (they will continue to cook). Remove the potatoes and cut into bite-sized pieces—usually halves and then eighths will do—carefully, as they may still be hot inside. Mix the potatoes with the sauce and enjoy!

Makes 4 servings.

POTATOES IN PARADISE

Single White Potato meets Dicey Green Avocado...you know this can only end with the two of them wrapping up in a tortilla and getting freaky.

1 Yukon gold potato
1 (10-inch) tortilla
1 avocado, diced
1/2 cup shredded lettuce
Salt, to taste

Stab the potato several times with a fork and get your frustrations out. Nuke for about 6 minutes, or until soft but not mushy. Cut into small cubes once cooled. Nuke the tortilla for 10 seconds to soften. Toss the potatoes, diced avocado, and lettuce onto the tortilla. Season with salt and wrap up.

Makes 1 serving.

PRETTY MUCH
THE BEST BURRITO

It's a Tatorito—a potato and a burrito mixed together. Get it?

1 sweet potato

1 (15-ounce) can pinto beans, drained and rinsed

2 large tortillas

1/2 cup salsa verde

2 tablespoons guacamole or vegan sour cream (or both, if you're feelin' feisty)

Poke some holes in the sweet potato with a fork. Nuke on high for 5 to 6 minutes, or until softened. Remove from the microwave, cut into small cubes, and set aside. Nuke the beans in a microwave-safe dish for 2 minutes and remove. One at a time, nuke the tortillas for 10 seconds to soften. To make the burritos, put half the potato cubes and half the beans in the middle of each tortilla. Top each with half of the salsa and half of the guacamole or sour cream. Eat.

Makes 2 servings.

CHILL-OUT CHILI FRIES

All work and no play will seriously *fry* your brain. Better take a study break with a plate of these delish fries!

1 bag frozen French fries

1 (15-ounce) can vegan chili or 2 cups homemade vegan chili

Place the French fries on a plate and nuke for 3 minutes, or until warm—or if you have a toaster oven, follow the directions on the package for cooking in a toaster oven. Empty the can of chili into a bowl and nuke for about 2 minutes, or until hot. Top the fries with chili and eat!

Makes 4 servings.

LAZY MAN'S CANDIED YAMS

Just like your mama's home cooking, if your mama were too lazy to actually cook. We won't slap you for eating it with your fingers, but you do have to get off your ass and cook it yourself.

1 sweet potato
Bottle of maple syrup

Stab the sweet potato with a fork multiple times to vent. Nuke on high for 5 minutes, or until tender. Let cool. Then pick the sweet 'tato up, squirt with some maple syrup, and eat like an apple.

Makes 1 serving.

IDAHO? NO, *YOU* DA HO POTATOES AU GRATIN

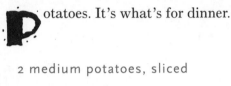otatoes. It's what's for dinner.

- 2 medium potatoes, sliced
- 1/2 cup nutritional yeast
- 1/2 cup soy milk
- 1 teaspoon salt
- 1 teaspoon garlic powder

Place the potato slices in a bowl and nuke for 3 minutes. Mix the remaining ingredients together until a sauce is formed. Top the potatoes with the sauce and microwave for 2–3 minutes or until the potatoes are tender.

Makes 2 servings.

TWICE-BAKED POTATOES

Finally—something more baked than your roommate.

1 medium baking potato

1 teaspoon chopped chives

1/4 cup vegan sour cream

1/2 cup shredded vegan cheddar cheese

Salt, pepper, and garlic powder, to taste

Stab the potato with a fork like it owes you money. Nuke for 5 minutes, or until potatoes are tender. Remove from the microwave and cut in half lengthwise when cool enough to handle. Use a large spoon to scoop out the inside of the potato, leaving the skin intact. Place the scoopings into a bowl. Stir the chives, sour cream, and cheese into the scooped-out part of the potato. Season with garlic powder, salt, and pepper and mix well. Nuke for 2 to 3 minutes, or until heated through. Scoop the mixture back into the potato skin and eat.

Makes 1 serving.

'TIS THE SEASON(ED) POTATO WEDGES

Look, dude, it may not be winter, but what the hell, try these anyway!

4–6 small potatoes, cut into thick wedges

3/4 cup vegan margarine, melted

Garlic-and-herb seasoned salt, to taste

Nuke the margarine in a small bowl until melted, about 90 seconds. Place the potato wedges on a microwave-safe plate and pour the melted margarine on top, making sure that each wedge is well coated. Sprinkle the seasoned salt over the wedges and nuke for about 2 minutes, or until tender. Let cool before eating.

Makes 4 servings.

ONE-HANDED TATER

Leaves the other hand free for the TV remote, mouse, or whatever.

1 potato
Ketchup and mustard, to taste

Stab the potato with a fork multiple times to vent. Nuke on high for 5 minutes or until tender. Let cool. Then pick up, add some ketchup and mustard, and eat like an apple.

Makes 1 serving.

PIZ-TATO

This super simple pizza/potato combo will be ready to devour before you can speed-dial the pizza delivery guy. Besides, isn't it just a *bit* shameful that you two are on a first-name basis?

1 large baking potato

3 tablespoons pizza or tomato sauce

1/2 cup shredded mozzarella-style vegan cheese

Stab the potato with a fork like you mean it. Microwave for about 6 minutes, or until squishy when lightly squeezed. Cut the potato in half and spoon pizza sauce over each half. Top with vegan cheese and pop back into the microwave for another minute, or until the cheese is melted.

Makes 1 serving.

CHEATER TATERS AND ONIONS

Whipping up a bowl of these taters and onions is even easier than paying the nerdy freshman downstairs to write your research paper.

1 potato, sliced

1/2 small onion, sliced

2 tablespoons vegan margarine

Salt and pepper, to taste

Put all the ingredients in a bowl. Cover and nuke for 4 minutes, or until the potatoes are tender.

Makes 1 serving.

MICRO-ECONOMICAL MICROWAVE POTATOES

When your supplies cannot meet your demands, there are always potatoes—cheap, filling, and delicious.

3 large potatoes, peeled and cubed

2 tablespoons vegan margarine

1 teaspoon onion powder

1 teaspoon garlic powder

1/2 teaspoon salt

1/8 teaspoon pepper

Combine all the ingredients in a dish and nuke for about 1 minute, until the margarine melts. Stir. Cook for 10 minutes more, stirring occasionally.

Makes 4 servings.

BEN FRANKLIN'S MISERLY MASHERS

When tuition's due, it's all about the Benjamins. Make your cash flow further with these penny-pinching potatoes

4 servings instant vegan mashed potatoes, cooked
    according to the package
1 tablespoon vegan bacon bits
1 tablespoon vegan cheese
1 tablespoon vegan sour cream
1 tablespoon chopped chives
Salt and pepper, to taste

Cook the instant potatoes according to the package, then mix together in all the other ingredients. There you go! It's best to add the bacon bits right before serving.

Makes 4 servings.

CRUNCHY MUNCHIES

For when it's late, and you've spent your last quarter on laundry.

1 tablespoon vegetable oil

1 potato, sliced paper thin (use the "cheese" part of a
   grater to do this)

Salt, to taste

Pour the oil into a plastic bag (a produce bag works well). Add the potato slices and shake to coat. Lightly coat a large dinner plate with oil. Arrange the potato slices in a single layer on the plate. Nuke for 3 to 5 minutes, or until lightly browned. Place the chips in a bowl and toss with salt. Let cool. Eat.

Makes 4 servings.

DESSERTS

If you're anything like us, you have an out-of-control sweet tooth that can flare up anytime, anywhere. It demands attention like a drunk girl at a party. Well, now you can satisfy yourself with some Ice Cream Pudding Pie or No-Bake Chocolate Cake. Feel free to share to score some brownie points with your RA.

DID YOU KNOW?

According to the American Dietetic Association, "Well-planned vegan and other types of vegetarian diets are appropriate for all stages of the life cycle, including during pregnancy, lactation, infancy, childhood, and adolescence."

CHOCOLATE DIP STICKS

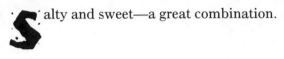 alty and sweet—a great combination.

1 (12-ounce) bag vegan chocolate chips

1 (10-ounce) bag pretzel rods

Chocolate or rainbow sprinkles (optional)

Line a tray with wax paper and set aside. Put the chocolate chips in a bowl and nuke for 1 minute. Stir. Heat for another 30 seconds, if necessary, and stir till smooth. Grab your pretzel rods and hold them over your bowl while, using a spoon, drizzling the melted chocolate over each pretzel. Hold over another bowl and sprinkle with sprinkles, if using. Place on the lined tray and put in the fridge until cool.

Makes 4 servings.

BACHELORETTE PARTY BERRIES

Have an engaged friend? Congratulate her on getting her 'MRS degree by making these bangin' berries. Then make her see how many she can fit in her mouth at once.

1 bag vegan chocolate chips
Strawberries
Wooden skewers

Put the chocolate chips in a bowl and nuke for 1 minute. Stir. Heat for another 30 seconds, if necessary, and stir until smooth. Dip the strawberries in the chocolate and place on aluminum foil to dry. Impale a few on each skewer and serve.

Makes 4 servings.

SPRING BREAK REMINDER PUDDING

Forget ambrosia—*this* is the food of the gods.

2 cups jarred mango, drained

1 teaspoon lime juice (from squirt bottle or fresh)

Shredded coconut and chopped pecans, to taste

Put the mango and lime juice in a blender and blend till smooth. Top with shredded coconut and/or pecan pieces and serve.

Makes 4 servings.

DUE DATES

Students live and die by deadlines. Now you can chew through yours like Godzilla in Tokyo.

1/2 cup raw nuts (try peanuts or cashews, but any will work)

2 tablespoons cinnamon

2 (8-ounce) bags pitted dates

Grind the nuts in a food processor or blender until chopped into small pieces. Add the cinnamon and pulse to combine. Set 13 to 15 dates aside, then add the rest to the blender. Grind again until the dates are about the same size as the nuts. Pour into a bowl and set aside. Cut the reserved dates down the long side in order to make room for the filling. Pinch small bits of the mixture together and stuff the dates. Eat.

Makes 4 servings.

FAKE BLONDES

We don't care if you highlight as long as your food is fake, too.

1/2 cup applesauce

2/3 cup sugar

1/4 cup canola oil

1 teaspoon vanilla extract

1 cup whole-wheat flour

4 tablespoons cocoa powder

1/2 teaspoon salt

1/2 cup vegan chocolate chips

Put the applesauce, sugar, canola oil, and vanilla in a large bowl and mix together well. In another bowl, mix together the flour, cocoa powder, and salt. Add the dry ingredients to the wet ingredients, stirring just until the dry ingredients are wet. Add the chocolate chips and stir a few times to incorporate. Pour into a baking dish that's been sprayed with cooking spray. Nuke for 4 to 5 minutes. Let cool to harden before cutting into bars.

Makes 4 servings.

GEORGIA PEACH COBBLER

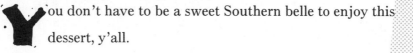**Y**ou don't have to be a sweet Southern belle to enjoy this dessert, y'all.

1 (15-ounce) can peaches with syrup

1/4 cup quick oats

1/4 cup corn flakes or granola (if using granola, make sure it's broken into small bits)

1/2 teaspoon cinnamon

1 tablespoon brown sugar

Remove 1 tablespoon of the syrup from the peaches and set aside. Mix together the oats and cereal or granola in a bowl. Put about 1/4 of the cereal mixture into a separate bowl, then add 1/3 of the peaches (including the syrup). Repeat the layers, ending with the cereal mixture on top. Sprinkle on the cinnamon and sugar and drizzle the reserved tablespoon of syrup on top. Nuke for about 2 minutes, until hot. Let cool for a few minutes before digging in.

Makes 4 servings.

MELON HEAD GRANITA

cross between a snow cone and a sorbet, this chill treat is just begging to be spooned.

4 cups seedless watermelon chunks

1/2 cup sugar

1 tablespoon lemon juice (fresh or from a squirt bottle)

Puree all the ingredients in a blender until smooth. Pour into a shallow, wide pan and freeze for 1 hour. Scrape the sides with a fork down to the bottom several times, then freeze for an additional hour. Repeat the scraping, and freeze for 1 more hour. Remove from the freezer, scrape with a fork, and serve immediately.

Makes 4 servings.

BANANA HAMMOCK BALLS

Full of tropical fruits and nuts, the only thing missing is a hammock. What were you thinking?

2 ripe bananas

1 cup shredded sweetened coconut

1/2 cup chopped dates

1 1/2 tablespoons cocoa powder

Mash the bananas in a bowl. Add the other ingredients and then form into balls. Nuke in the microwave for 1 minute, or until heated through.

Makes 4 servings.

ICE CREAM FRIZZLE DRIZZLE

Best to use at our favorite type of bar—a vegan ice cream sundae bar!

1 cup frozen berries

1 tablespoon powdered sugar

1/2 teaspoon dried mint

1/8 teaspoon vanilla

Blend all the ingredients together in a blender. Pour on top of ice cream, sorbet, cake, or another sweet of your choice, and serve.

Makes 4 servings.

NOON IN CANCUN FROZEN "YOGURT"

Reminisce about that spring break trip to Mexico with a bowl of fruity, cool, and creamy goodness.

1/2 cup soy yogurt (your favorite fruit flavor)
1/4 cup orange juice
1/4 cup canned pineapple chunks, drained
1/4 cup canned orange slices, drained
Sprinkle of coconut

Put the soy yogurt, orange juice, pineapple, and oranges in a blender and blend until smooth. Pour into a bowl and stir in the coconut. Freeze for at least 1 hour before eating.

Makes 4 servings.

CREAMY BANANA-WAFER PUDDING

ny recipe with pudding is an automatic crowd pleaser.

3/4 cup vegan vanilla wafers

2 bananas, sliced

1 package vegan pudding

1 1/2 cups cold soy or almond milk

Put the wafers in the bottom of a 9 × 9-inch dish and top with half of the banana slices. Prepare the pudding by placing the dry pudding mix and the cold soy or almond milk in a blender and beating gently until smooth. Pour the pudding on top of the banana-wafer "crust." Let set in the fridge for a couple of hours. Top with extra banana slices and serve.

Makes 4 servings.

FOOD OF THE GODDESSES

Pamper yourself with these tasty morsels.

3 1/2 cups vegan cake or cookie crumbs (just crumble
   some soft cookies or cake)

1 1/2 cups powdered sugar

5 1/2 tablespoons vegan margarine

6 tablespoons orange juice

1/3 cup shredded coconut

Stir together the cake crumbs and powdered sugar in a large
bowl. Add the margarine and orange juice. Mix well, then form
balls about 1 inch across. Roll the balls in the shredded coconut,
place on a large plate, and chill in the refrigerator for an hour,
until firm.

Makes 4 servings.

MIAMI BEACH PUDDING

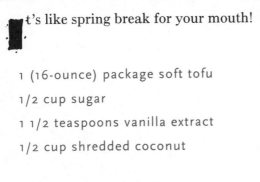

It's like spring break for your mouth!

1 (16-ounce) package soft tofu

1/2 cup sugar

1 1/2 teaspoons vanilla extract

1/2 cup shredded coconut

Whip the tofu, sugar, and vanilla extract in a blender until stiff and creamy. In a bowl, fold the coconut into the tofu mixture. Pour the pudding into parfait glasses or individual dessert bowls and chill. For an extra treat, serve topped with chocolate sauce.

Makes 4 servings.

POSEUR PINEAPPLE PIE

Looks like pineapple pie, but don't be fooled by this suspiciously docile dessert. Underneath it all, it's just fruit trying to be something it's not.

1/2 tablespoon cornstarch

1 (20-ounce) can crushed pineapple, refrigerated and
  undrained

1 cup fresh blueberries

1/2 pint fresh strawberries, cut up

1 (20-ounce) can sliced peaches, drained

1 vegan pie crust

Put the cornstarch and 3 tablespoons of the cold pineapple juice in a dish and mix together well. Add the rest of the pineapple juice, along with the pineapple, and nuke for 5 minutes, or until bubbling and thickened. Set aside. Arrange the blueberries, strawberries, and peaches in the crust and cover with the pineapple sauce. Refrigerate for at least 1 hour before serving.

Makes 6 servings.

CHEAPSKATE DATES

A small price to pay for a big reward. Don't you wish all of your dates were this cheap and easy?

1/2 (8-ounce) container vegan cream cheese
1/4 cup powdered sugar
2 tablespoons orange juice
1 box whole pitted dates
Powdered sugar, optional

Beat together the cream cheese, powdered sugar, and orange juice in a bowl. Cut each date down the middle and stuff the cream cheese mixture into the date and refrigerate for at least 30 minutes. Dust with powdered sugar before serving, if you wanna get fancy.

Makes 4 servings.

CHOCO-NANNER PARFAIT

Parfait is French for perfect. Say that to those study-abroad hotties over at the languages building and see how they swoon.

1 package vegan pudding (vanilla or chocolate)

1 1/2 cups soy milk

1 cup crushed vegan cookies or graham crackers

2 large bananas, sliced

Vegan chocolate chips

Mix the pudding with the milk. Refrigerate for 10 minutes. Layer some of the cookies, banana slices, and pudding in a tall glass. Top with some chocolate chips and refrigerate for 1 hour.

Makes 4 servings.

BLUEBERRY PIE DUMP CAKE

Like with dumpster diving, all of the good stuff is always at the bottom.

- 1 (21-ounce) can blueberry pie filling
- 1 (8 1/2-ounce) can crushed pineapple, sweetened and undrained
- 1 (9-ounce) package vegan yellow cake mix (try Duncan Hines—many are vegan)
- 1/3 cup vegan margarine, melted
- 1/2 cup coarsely chopped walnuts or pecans

Spread blueberry pie filling evenly into a cake dish, then spoon pineapple (including the juice) on top of it. Sprinkle cake mix evenly over the fruit, then sprinkle the nuts on top. Drizzle melted margarine as evenly as possible over all. Set the cake dish on a book to raise it a little nearer the center of the microwave, then nuke uncovered for 10 minutes. Give the dish a quarter turn twice during cooking. Mixture should be boiling throughout. Set dish out on flat surface and allow to cool before serving.

Makes 6 servings.

BREAKUP PUDDING

Nothing mends a broken heart quite like sitting in bed in your pajamas, watching hours of reality TV, and eating an entire bowl of this chocolate pudding.

1 pack firm silken tofu, crumbled
10 tablespoons sugar
8 tablespoons unsweetened cocoa powder
2 1/2 teaspoons vanilla extract
Pinch of salt

Blend all ingredients in a food processor or blender until creamy and thick. Chill.

Makes 4 servings.

NO-BAKE CHOCOLATE CAKE

No oven? No problem. Help yourself to some Easy Bake lovin' straight from your microwave oven.

Nonstick vegan margarine spray

3 tablespoons vegan margarine, softened

1/4 cup sugar

1/4 cup banana, mashed

1 teaspoon vanilla extract

1/4 cup soy milk

1/2 cup flour

2 tablespoons cocoa powder

1/4 teaspoon baking powder

Dash of salt

Spray a medium bowl with nonstick spray and set aside. In a separate bowl, combine the margarine, sugar, banana, vanilla extract, and soy milk; stir together. Combine the flour, cocoa powder, baking powder, and salt in another bowl. Stir the dry mixture into the wet one until smooth, then pour into the greased bowl. Cover and cook in the microwave on high for 2 to 2 1/2 minutes, or until cake springs back when touched. To serve, let the cake cool five minutes. When it's cooled, cover the bowl with a plate and turn both bowl and plate upside down so the cake falls onto the plate.

Makes 4 servings.

MALLOW-NUT TRUFFLES

All your favorite snack foods in one bite. It doesn't get any better than that.

- 1 cup plain popped popcorn
- 1 cup vegan marshmallow topping (we like Smucker's and Ricemellow)
- 1 cup salted peanuts
- 1 pound vegan semisweet chocolate, broken into pieces

Coat a baking pan with oil and/or cooking spray. Gently mix the popcorn, marshmallow topping, and peanuts together and form into little mounds on the pan. Put the chocolate pieces in a bowl and nuke for 1 minute. Stir. Heat for another 30 seconds, if necessary, and stir until smooth. Pour the melted chocolate over each little mound, covering completely. Refrigerate until chocolate is set.

Makes 4 servings.

COUCH SURFER SPONGE PUDDING

Super smooth banana pudding that's easy to make and easy to swallow—unlike the fact that your couch-crashing buddy won't get off your futon.

1/4 cup vegan margarine

1/4 cup sugar

1/4 cup banana, mashed

2 tablespoons soy milk

1/2 cup self-rising flour

In a medium bowl, mix together the margarine and sugar until smooth. Add the banana and soy milk and, while stirring, slowly add the flour, mixing until all the ingredients are well blended. Cover and nuke for 3 1/2 minutes, or until the pudding is slightly congealed. Eat.

Makes 4 servings.

LOCO-COCOA SNACK CAKE

Crazy fast and delicious.

1 1/2 cups all-purpose flour

1 cup sugar

1 teaspoon baking soda

1/2 cup unsweetened cocoa powder

1/2 teaspoon salt

1 cup water

1/2 cup vegetable oil

2 tablespoons white vinegar

2 teaspoons vanilla extract

Combine the flour, sugar, baking soda, cocoa powder, and salt in a bowl. Combine the remaining ingredients in a separate bowl, then stir into the flour mixture. Microwave on high for 6 to 7 minutes, rotating 1/4 turn twice, until a fork comes out clean when inserted in the center. Let cool for 10 minutes.

Makes 4 servings.

CHOCOLATE DORM CAKE

Need to find common ground with someone? This cake is a great way to start—there's no problem that chocolate cannot solve.

Super moist chocolate cake mix (Duncan Hines has vegan options—follow directions for a super moist chocolate cake)

1 (8-ounce) container vegan cream cheese

1/4 cup sugar

1 teaspoon vanilla

1 1/2 teaspoons egg replacer mixed with 2 tablespoons water

1 (12-ounce) bag vegan chocolate chips

Pour 3/4 of the cake batter into a casserole dish, then set aside. In a bowl, stir together the cream cheese, sugar, vanilla, and egg replacer until smooth. Fold in the chocolate chips. Spread the cream cheese mixture evenly over the batter in the casserole dish. Pour remaining cake batter into casserole dish. Cook uncovered in microwave for 15 minutes. Rotate the cake while cooking. Watch closely and make sure the cake is cooking evenly. Let cool 5 or 10 minutes. Flip cake onto plate and serve.

Makes 4 servings.

MARSHMALLOW MADNESS SQUARES

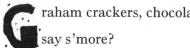raham crackers, chocolate, and marshmallows. Need we say s'more?

30 graham crackers, divided into squares

1 (12-ounce) package vegan semisweet chocolate chips

6 tablespoons vegan margarine

1 (12.25-ounce) jar vegan marshmallow topping (we like Smucker's and Ricemellow)

1 (13-ounce) box puffed rice cereal

Spray a 13 × 9-inch pan with cooking spray. Place 15 graham squares on the bottom of the pan, overlapping slightly. Set aside. Put the chocolate chips and 2 tablespoons of the margarine in a bowl and nuke for 2 minutes, then stir until melted. Spread half of the melted chocolate over the graham squares.

Nuke the remaining 4 tablespoons of margarine in a bowl for 45 seconds, or until melted. Add the marshmallow topping and stir until smooth. Add the cereal and mix to coat.

Press the cereal mixture firmly over the graham squares in the pan. Drizzle with the remaining melted chocolate. Immediately top with the remaining 15 graham squares. Cool and then dive in!

Makes 10 servings.

PINK PRINCESS PIE

Charm those snotty girls on the campus events committee with this sweet and creamy dessert while you make your case for allowing a vegan bake sale during welcome week.

1 (12-ounce) can pink lemonade concentrate

2 1/2 cups soy ice cream

Vegan graham cracker pie crust

Blend the lemonade concentrate for 30 seconds in the blender. Spoon in the ice cream, and blend until combined. Pour into the crust and freeze overnight.

Makes 4 servings.

SNOWBALLS FROM HELL

The odds of these peachy keen popsicles lasting once your roommates know about them? A snowball's chance in hell. Like your odds of getting into your first choice for grad school.

- 1 1/2 cups canned peaches, drained
- 1/4 cup peach preserves
- 1 tablespoon sugar
- 1 tablespoon coconut flakes

Put everything in a blender and blend. Place 2 tablespoons of the mixture in each cube of an ice cube tray. Freeze until almost firm, then insert a toothpick in each one and freeze the rest of the way.

Makes 4 servings.

SCREAMING PUDDING PIE

One bite of this, and your taste buds—and maybe your crush—will be screaming for more.

1 cup cold soy milk
1 cup vegan ice cream (any flavor), softened
1 package vegan pudding
Graham cracker crust

Mix together the milk and ice cream in a large bowl. Add the pudding and mix for 1 to 2 minutes. Pour into the crust and refrigerate for a couple of hours.

Makes 4 servings.

SHAKE-AND-MAKE FRO YO

Don't settle for that diseased dairy crap from the ice cream stand down the street. Make your own!

1 gallon-sized plastic resealable bag

3–4 pounds of ice cubes

6 tablespoons rock salt

2 tablespoons sugar

1 cup vanilla soy milk

1/2 tablespoon vanilla extract

1 pint-sized plastic resealable bag

Vegan cones

Fill the gallon-sized plastic bag half full with ice. Add the rock salt and set aside. Pour the sugar, soy milk, and vanilla into the pint-sized bag and seal. Place the pint-sized plastic bag inside the gallon-sized plastic bag and seal. Shake the bag for 5 to 7 minutes. Remove the pint-sized bag from the larger bag. Use scissors to cut away a corner from the pint-sized bag, then squeeze the soy ice cream into the cones, soft-serve style. Top with sprinkles, if desired.

Makes 4 servings.

NOTE:

Use oven mitts to prevent your hands from getting too cold.

COMFORT PUDDING

I promise, this pudding will distract you from checking your cell every 10 minutes to see if he texted you.

1/3 cup cocoa powder

3/4 cup sugar

1/4 teaspoon salt

1/4 cup cornstarch

3 cups soy milk

1 1/2 teaspoons vanilla extract

Put the cocoa powder, sugar, salt, cornstarch, and soy milk in a dish and nuke for 5 minutes, stirring halfway through. Remove from the microwave and stir in the vanilla. Chill before serving.

Makes 4 servings.

INDEX BY INGREDIENT